EVERY PERSON'S GUIDE TO HANUKKAH

RONALD H. ISAACS

JASON ARONSON INC.
Northvale, New Jersey
Jerusalem

This book was set in 12 pt. Garamond Light by Alabama Book Composition of Deatsville, Al, and printed and bound by Book-mart Press, Inc. of North Bergen, NJ.

10 9 8 7 6 5 4 3 2 1

Library of Congress Cataloguing-in-Publication Data

Isaacs, Ronald H.
    Every person's guide to Hanukkah/ by Ronald H. Isaacs.
        p. cm.
    Includes bibliographical references and index.
    ISBN 0-7657-6044-4 (alk. paper)
    1. Hanukkah. I. title.
  BM695. H3173 2000
  296.4'35—dc21   98–21765
                                                CIP

Printed in the United States of America. Jason Aronson Inc. offers books and cassettes. For information and catalog write to Jason Aronson Inc., 230 Livingston Street, Northvale, NJ 07647-1726, or visit our website: http://www.aronson.com

CONTENTS

PREFACE

Hanukkah, although considered a minor holiday rabbinically speaking, is one of the most widely observed Jewish holidays. Its celebration is joyful, centering on lights, presents, games, and tasty foods. This post-biblical festival of lights is annually celebrated for eight days, beginning on the twenty-fifth of the Hebrew month of Kislev. It commemorates the historic struggle of the Jews against pagan forces at the time of the religious persecutions by the Greco-Syrians, a struggle which proved decisive in forming the character of the Jewish people. The great Maccabean victories eventually led to the religious freedom and national independence of the Jews, inspiring many subsequent generations to face persecution with triumphant courage.

The lighting of the candles on the eight days of Hanukkah, one on the first day and one more on each succeeding day, is likened in the Talmud with the miracle of the cruse of oil. When the Hasmoneans prevailed against their heathen foe, they found in the

Temple only one undefiled cruse of oil, with the seal of
the High Priest. This cruse contained sufficient oil for
one day's lighting of the Temple Menorah, but, miraculously, its oil burned for eight days. The following year,
they designated these eight days for giving thanks and
praise to God. The rededication of the Temple after its
defilement by pagan worship of Greek gods occurred in
the year 165 before the common era.

Hanukkah has encouraged many a small group to
fight against injustice and oppressions. It has been a
source of inspiration in the movement to liberate the
Land of Israel and establish it as an independent state. It
has also stimulated the Jew to withstand assimilation and
the temptation of false gods, to champion the ideals of
one's heritage in the midst of an overwhelming majority,
and to stress Jewish culture in the face of a vast culture
that seeks to engulf him.

This book presents the history of the festival of
Hanukkah, its rituals, customs, laws, legends, stories,
songs, and creative celebration. I hope that using this
book will help to shed bright light for all eight days of
your Hanukkah celebration. Hag Hanukkah Sameach!

Ronald H. Isaacs

HANUKKAH
IN JEWISH HISTORY

IN THE BIBLE

Hanukkah is the most historically documented of all of the Jewish holidays. We have early sources for the story in the First and Second Books of the Maccabees and in the works of the historian Josephus. We have somewhat later accounts in the Talmud, and there is even a medieval work called *The Scroll of Antiochus* which is modeled after the biblical Book of Esther. Each of these accounts adds additional details to the story of Hanukkah and its origins.

Before examining these sources in greater detail, the common version of the Hanukkah story will be reviewed.

In the fourth century before the common era, Alexander the Great, with his Greek armies, conquered the Near East including Israel. After his death, his empire split apart and his domain was divided up by his warring generals, Seleucis and Ptolemy, into the Seleucid (Asia

Minor and Syria) and Ptolemaic (Egypt) kingdoms. Greece was left in the hands of General Antigonus. Meanwhile, at the other end of the Mediterranean, Rome had conquered Italy and commenced to make her presence felt.

For more than a century after the breakup of Alexander's empire, Palestine was ruled by the Ptolemies of Egypt. The Ptolemaic kings collected taxes but did permit the Jews religious and culture freedom. Although Hellenization was not enforced, it went on nevertheless, and Jews learned Greek and took on Greek names. Soon, the Jews became internally divided between those who saw no danger in Hellenization and those more conservative, called the Pietists or Hasidim, who felt that Greek influence would cause the total assimilation of the Jewish people.

Thirty-four years before the Maccabean revolt, the Seleucid Emperor Antiochus III of Syria took Palestine away from the Egyptian king. Initially, Antiochus III (who is the father of the Antiochus of our Hanukkah story) continued the lenient policies of the Egyptians. However, upon seeing the rise of Rome on the horizon, he decided that he could defeat Rome with a unified empire behind him. Thus began an intense program of Hellenization which included the erection of Greek statues and idols in all public places, including the Jerusalem Temple.

Antiochus IV, who next inherited the Syrian throne, was known as Antiochus Epiphanes ("god manifest"). He decided to force the Jews, together with all other peoples over whom he reigned, to follow the Greek religion and no other. The Jews were not allowed to live as the Torah taught, and they were ordered to worship

Greek gods and to behave like the Greeks in other ways as well. Sabbath observance, Torah study, and circumcision were banned and were all punishable by death. Life in Jerusalem became a nightmare.

Led by the aged priest Mattathias, who lived in the town of Modin near Jerusalem, the Jews decided to rebel and fight the Syrians. Mattathias, together with his five sons and other brave volunteers, began fighting against the mighty and superior Syrian armies.

When, about a year later, Mattathias died, his son Judah (called the "Maccabee") took his place as the leader. Because Judah was a very clever general, he and his small force were able to fight for three years and, in the end, defeat the Syrians.

After his victory, Judah and his men went into the Temple in Jerusalem and cleansed it of all the Greek gods and idols that the Syrians had placed there. When it was purified, they wanted to kindle the large menorah (candelabrum), but they were unable to find a container of oil bearing the seal of the High Priest. Finally, as the common version of the story goes, someone did find a small cruse of oil, which, however, was enough for only one day. But God performed a miracle: The small jar of oil burned for eight days, by which time more of the pure oil had been prepared. The miracle, coming on the heels of the military victory, cheered the people greatly and they celebrated in joyous thanksgiving.

To remind ourselves of this wonderful miracle and to keep alive the feeling that we Jews are always ready to fight for our right to freely worship God, we light candles on each successive Hanukkah night.

FIRST AND SECOND BOOK OF MACCABEES

The Maccabean exploits are told in the two books of the Maccabees, the last books of the Apocrypha. They are filled with stories of defiant martyrdom during a period of fifteen years and contain descriptions of Mattathias and his five sons: Jochanan, Simeon, Judah, Elazar, and Jonathan.

The First Book of the Maccabees covers the period of forty years from the accession of Antiochus Epiphanes (175 B.C.E.) to the death of Simon Maccabee (135 B.C.E.). The events are chronicled with intense interest and sympathy, with direct and objective style.

When Judah took over after Mattathias's death, the nature of the rebels' activities changed. The third chapter of I Maccabees describes the major battles leading to the repossession of the Temple. Here is an excerpt of the poem of praise to Judah:

> And his son Judah, who was called Maccabee, rose up in
> his stead.
> And all his brothers helped him.
> And all those who were adherents to his father,
> And gladly they fought Israel's battle.
> He extended the glory of his people.
> And put on a breastplate as a giant.
> And girded on his weapons of war.
> He set battles in array, with the sword.
> He protected the army
> And he was like a lion in his deeds,
> And as a lion's whelp roaring for prey
> He pursued the lawless, seeking them out,

And destroyed those who troubled his people.
The lawless lost heart for fear of him,
And all the workers of lawlessness were troubled;
And deliverance prospered in his hand.
He angered many kings,
And made Jacob glad with his acts.
And his memory is blessed forever.
He went about among the cities of Judah,
And destroyed the ungodly thereout,
And turned away wrath from Israel.
And he was renowned to the ends of the earth,
And gathered together those who were perishing.

(*I Maccabees* 3:1–9)

I Maccabees (4:36–59) states that Judah Maccabee, after defeating Lysias, entered Jerusalem and purified the Temple. The altar that had been defiled was demolished and a new one was built. Judah then made new holy vessels (among them a candelabrum, an altar of incense, a table, and curtains) and set the twenty-fifth of Kislev as the date for the rededication of the Temple. The day coincided with the third anniversary of the proclamation of the restrictive edicts of Antiochus Epiphanes in which he had decreed that the idolatrous sacrifices should be offered on a platform erected upon the altar. The altar was to be reconsecrated with the renewal of the daily sacrificial service, accompanied by song, the playing of musical instruments, the chanting of Hallel, and the offering of sacrifices. No mention of any special festival customs is made. The celebrations lasted for eight days and Judah decreed that they be designated as days of rejoicing for future generations. Following is a narrative

from the Book of Maccabees of the rededication of the
Jerusalem Temple:

> They took whole stones, according to the Law, and built
> a new altar after the fashion of the former; and they built
> the sanctuary, and the inner parts of the Temple, and
> hallowed the courts. And they made the vessels new,
> and they brought the candlestick, the altar of burnt-
> offerings and of incense, and the table, into the Temple.
> And they burned incense upon the altar, and they lit the
> lamps that were upon the candlestick in order to give
> light in the Temple. And they set loaves upon the table,
> and hung up the curtains, and finished all the works
> which they had undertaken. . . . And they rose up early
> in the morning on the twenty-fifth of Kislev. At the cor-
> responding time and on the corresponding day on which
> the gentiles had profaned it, on that very day it was
> rededicated afresh, with songs and harps and lutes, and
> with cymbals. . . . They celebrated the dedication of the
> altar for eight days, and offered burnt offerings with glad-
> ness, and sacrificed a sacrifice of deliverance and praise.
> And they decked the front of the Temple with crowns of
> gold and small shields, and dedicated afresh the gates
> and the chambers, and furnished them with doors. . . .
> Judah and his brothers and the whole congregation of
> Israel ordained that the days of the dedication of the altar
> should be kept in their season year by year for eight
> days, from the twenty-fifth of the month Kislev, with
> gladness and joy. (*I Maccabees* 4:47–60)

The Second Book of Maccabees was written in Greek,
probably around 120 years before the common era (forty
years after the event). It has been conjectured that it was

probably written as a polemic to encourage the large Jewish community living in Egypt to join in the celebration of Hanukkah. Following is its account, which shows the origins of the Maccabean conflict as a civil problem, with Jewish factions competing for control of national religious practice:

> After Seleucus died, Antiochus Epiphanes ascended the throne. Jason, brother of Onias the High Priest, supplanted his brother by promising the King three hundred and sixty talents of silver and eighty talents from other sources. In addition, he was promised another fifty if he was given permission to build a gymnasium and change the name of the city of Jerusalem to Antiochia. The king agreed and Jason took over. He immediately started to convert his countrymen to the Greek way of life. He broke down the traditional way of life and introduced new customs forbidden by the law. He set up the gymnasium right in the Temple Citadel and introduced the finest young men to the wearing of the Petsus hat. The passion for adopting Greek customs rose to such heights that the priests would neglect their Temple service in favor of unlawful exercise, running from their duties as soon as a call came for discus throwing. (*I Maccabees* 4)

Here is the Second Book of Maccabees account of the rededication of the Temple. It shares details with the first account, but with an interesting twist:

> Maccabeus with his men, led by God, recovered the Temple and the city of Jerusalem. He demolished the altars erected by the heathens in the public square and

their sacred precincts as well. When they had purified
the sanctuary they constructed another altar, then striking fire from flints, they offered the lights, and the
shewbread. . . . The sanctuary was purified on the
twenty-fifth of Kislev. . . . This joyful celebration went
on for eight days. It was like Sukkot, for they recalled
how only a short time before they had kept the festival
while living like animals in the mountains, and so they
carried lulavim and etrogim, and they chanted hymns to
God who had triumphantly led them to the purification
of the Temple. A measure was passed by the public
assembly that the entire Jewish people should observe
these days every year. (*II Maccabees* 10:1–8)

In this account, unlike in that of the First Book of
Maccabees, we are now told that Hanukkah is an eight-
day celebration. Furthermore, we are told that Hanukkah began as a second celebration of the eight-day
festival of Sukkot. The reason given is that the Jews had
been fugitives not long before, and when it was time to
celebrate Sukkot, they had not been able to properly
observe the holiday. Having Sukkot later in the year
would recompense them for what they had missed.

THE MIRACLE OF THE FIRE

The story of the ancient miracle of the fire is given
prominence in the letter allegedly written by Judah
Maccabee to the Egyptian Jews. This letter prefixes the
Second Book of Maccabees. The Egyptian Jews were
admonished to observe Hanukkah as "the feast of Tab-
ernacles and the fire which was given to us when

Nehemiah offered sacrifices after he had built the Temple and the altar." An explanatory paragraph follows in which the story of the miracle is related. Nehemiah is said to have sent some priests to locate the celestial fire of the first Temple. The fire had been hidden in a cave at the command of the prophet Jeremiah, and the hiding place was to remain a secret until the time when God would choose to restore the people to the Holy Land. Nehemiah, now certain that the time of redemption had arrived, dispatched some priests in search of the cave. The priests located it but found in it water and no fire. However, when the sun came out, a great fire was kindled, and all of those present marveled at the wondrous miracle.

According to the assertion of Rabbi Abraham Bloch, the miracle story of the fire was given prominence because the prime objective of the author was to prove the sanctity of the Second Temple and its superiority over Onias's temple in Egypt. The celestial fire was to be forever a reminder of divine intervention and a sign of heavenly approval for the Second Temple.

This story of the miracle of the fire is the appearance of the first recorded account of a miracle linked with the festival of Hanukkah. Incidentally, the term "miracle" is not mentioned in the Second Book of Maccabees but was first popularized in the rabbinic tradition of the Talmud.

HANNAH AND HER SEVEN SONS

There is a most moving story told in the Second Book of Maccabees (Chapter 7) of seven brothers who were seized along with their mother, Hannah, by Antiochus Epiphanes, presumably shortly after the beginning of the religious persecutions in 166 B.C.E. This family was ordered to prove their obedience to the king by partaking of swine's flesh. Every one of them refused to do so.

Next, a high Syrian officer set up a Greek idol and commanded each of Hannah's sons to bow to it. He began with the oldest son, who refused. Then, as each son in turn refused to bow down to the idol, he was sent off to be tortured and killed.

When Hannah was appealed to by the king to spare the youngest child's life by prevailing upon him to comply, she urged the child instead to follow in the path of his brothers. He was also sent off to die. Shortly thereafter, she herself died.

It was acts of sacrifice of this kind that inspired the Jews to fight for and to defend their religion, their most prized possession.

A condensed version of the story of Hannah and her seven sons appears in the Talmudic tractate of Gittin 57b. In many parts of the non-Jewish world, shrines have been established to the memory of the seven martyred children and their devout mother, Salome. The name given them in non-Jewish tradition is Maccabean, perhaps because of the Maccabean struggles of that period. In some Jewish sources, the name Miriam is given to their mother.

THE SCROLL OF ANTIOCHUS

The Scroll of Antiochus is the first rabbinic interpretation of Hanukkah. The scroll has been handed down in several Aramaic versions, probably dating from the late Talmudic period from the second to the fifth centuries of the common era. There are two interesting features of the scroll in comparison with the Books of the Maccabees. First of all, Judah Maccabee is downgraded in importance. He is said to have been killed early in the encounter with Bacchides, whereupon Mattathias, his father, assumed the military leadership and finally proceeded to cleanse and purify the Temple. Another striking feature is the omission of the story of the dedication of the altar.

According to Rabbi Abraham Bloch, the Scroll of Antiochus reflects the views of the early Hasidim and the subsequent generation of rabbis during the rebellion against Rome. Wars are to be sanctioned only if they are waged in defense of faith and life. The attainment of political ends, even the defense of independence, does not warrant bloodshed. There is good reason to assume that Judah Maccabee lost the backing of the Hasidim prior to his last battle, and thus his lesser role in the scroll. On the other hand, Judah's father, Mattathias, was said to have sparked the rebellion, his only objective being freedom of religion. That met with the wholehearted support of the Hasidim, and that is why Mattathias, along with his sons Jochanan and Eleazar, are given more prominent roles in the scroll of Antiochus.

Furthermore, the author of the Scroll of Antiochus ignored the dedication of the altar because it was linked historically to Judah Maccabee. The elimination of Judah's part in the rebellion left the story of the dedication untold.

In the story from the Scroll of Antiochus, as the Jews are reconsecrating their Temple, they find a vessel bearing the seal of the High Priest dating back to the time of the Prophet Samuel. By a miracle, the oil, which was sufficient in quantity for only one day, burned in the lamp for eight days. And this is why Hanukkah, the festival commemorating the reconsecration of the Temple, is celebrated for eight days.

In spite of the profound influence of the Scroll of Antiochus, it was never officially sanctioned by the talmudic authorities nor was there a special effort made to preserve it. Its many historical inaccuracies might have weighted heavily against it. The rabbis also looked askance at the publication of any written book outside of the canon.

Some communities (including Italian synagogues) choose to read the Scroll of Antiochus during Hanukkah. The scroll can also be found in various prayerbooks.

THE STORY OF JUDITH

In addition to the First and the Second Books of the Maccabees, the Apocrypha contains the Book of Judith, which tells the story of a beautiful Jewish woman who single-handedly saved the Jewish town of Bethulia during the Hasmonean revolt. The basic story is as follows:

> Nebuchadnezzar, the king of Assyria, reigned in Nineveh after having defeated Arphaxad, the king of Media. Nebuchadnezzar then sent Holofornes, his own commander-in-chief, on a campaign of conquest, in the

course of which he overran all the countries from the border of Persia to Sidon and Tyre. When he reached the valley of Esdraelon before the narrow pass leading to Judea and Jerusalem, he found that by order of the high priest in Jerusalem all the passes had been occupied by the Jews living in the fortified mountain pass towns of Bethulia and Betomesthaim. At this, Holofernes summoned a council, and as a result, he ordered that Achior, the Ammonite chief, who had spoken confidently of the victorious power of Israel so long as they remained faithful to God, be sent to the Jews of Bethuliah. Holofernes then laid siege to the town. After a month, when there was no water left in Bethulia and its leaders had already decided to open the gates to the enemy, there suddenly appeared a widow named Judith. She was of the tribe of Simeon and a resident of Bethuliah; she was young and beautiful, righteous and wealthy. With the permission of the leaders of the town, she went down to the camp of Holofernes, who, attracted by her beauty and wisdom, invited her to a feast. When Holofernes fell asleep, overcome by wine, Judith took his dagger, decapitated him, and handed his head to her maid, who returned with her to Bethulia. Now deprived of their commander-in-chief by Judith's courageous deed, the panic-stricken Assyrian soldiers fled.

There are many obscure elements in the story. Some have maintained that the story is simply an allegory. Others assert that it is a historical novel written in the days of the Hasmoneans to inspire courage. Set in the Babylonian period, the Book of Judith seems to have no connection with Hanukkah. How it came to be connected is unclear, but medieval Hebrew versions of the story place it in the context of the Hasmonean revolt. Recent scholarship explains the connection of Hanukkah and the book by dating the writing of it to the time of the Maccabees. The story is used to explain the custom of eating cheese on Hanukkah.

The story of Judith has inspired a long list of artistic representations, including those of Michelangelo, who painted figures of Judith and her maid on the Sistine Chapel ceiling.

HISTORICAL TIME LINE

The following is an historical time line of the events that led to the unfolding of the festival of Hanukkah. You may wish to use it as a handy reference.

325 B.C.E. Death of Alexander the Great

Empire divided between Ptolemy (Egypt) and Seleucus (Syria)
Israel under control of Ptolemies and then Seleucids
Jewish life generally harsh under Greeks
Assimilation and adoption of Hellenistic cult; resisted by Hasidim

246–221 B.C.E. (Ptolemy III)

Refusal by High Priest, Chonyo to pay tribute
Appointment of Hellenistic Joseph as High Priest
Joseph uses position for personal gain; enforces taxes with aid of army

Succession of corrupt High Priests and Temple officials
Collaborated with king to extort and persecute Jews

175 B.C.E. Antiochus IV
succeeded the Seleucid throne

Brutal imposition of Hellenistic culture:
    Observance of the Jewish Sabbath banned,
    Circumcision outlawed,
    Desecration of Torah scrolls and its study outlawed,
    Confiscation and burning of Jewish books,
    Execution of those professing to be a Jew,
    Jews forced to eat pork from sacrifices and worship
        Greek deities,
    Jewish brides forced to submit to Syrian officers before
        marriage
Jerusalem Temple pillaged, with sacrifices of pigs to
    Greek gods
Temple converted into a place of harlotry

167 B.C.E. Revolt against Antiochus

Mattathias the Hasmonean and his five sons at Modin
    (Simon, Judah, Jonathan, Yochanan, and Elazar)
Guerilla campaign against Syrians led by Judah the
    Maccabee

165 B.C.E. Liberation of the Temple
on the 25th of Kislev

Miracle of the oil

164 B.C.E. Antiochus V
rescinds edict banning Judaism

Maccabean wars continue both in Israel and outside
Seleucid monarchy weakens

141 B.C.E. Jewish independence
recognized by Syria

Simon appointed Prince and High Priest pro tem

63 B.C.E. Judea conquered by Romans

66–73 C.E. Revolt of the Zealots
70 C.E. Destruction of Second Temple by Romans
135 C.E. Bar Kochba Revolt

IN RABBINIC LITERATURE

The Talmud bears a number of passages which describe
Hanukkah practice. For example, the miracle of oil
which we commemorate by lighting the hanukkiah is
recorded in the following passage:

> What is Hanukkah? The Rabbis learned: When the
> Greeks entered the Temple they defiled all the oils that
> were in it. When the Hasmonean dynasty triumphed and
> defeated the Syrian Greeks, the Kohanim searched, but
> found only one container of oil, which had been laid
> aside. But there was only enough oil in it to light the
> Temple menorah for one day. A miracle occurred with it,

and they lit with it for eight days. The following year, they fixed and established these days as festivals of praise and thanksgiving. (*Talmud Shabbat* 21b)

According to the medieval commentator Rashi, the reference to "praise and thanksgiving" refers to the recital of the Hallel Psalms of praise, which are to be recited at each of the morning services during the festival of Hanukkah. The expression "thanksgiving" refers to the paragraph "al hanissim" ("for the miracles"), which is added during the Amidah prayer and the Grace after the meal.

Here are several additional passages (*Talmud Shabbat* 21b–24b) which describe additional Hanukkah practice in rabbinic times:

Our rabbis taught: The mitzvah of Hanukkah is for each family to light one lamp. The one who wishes to beautify this mitzvah fully should light one lamp for each person in the family. The one who wishes to beautify this mitzvah completely—Bet Shammai taught that one should light eight lights on the first night, and one less each following day. Bet Hillel taught that one should light one light on the first day and more each following day. . . .

Rabbi Yose ben Abin and Rabbi Jose ben Abida explained their positions. One taught: Bet Shammai's reason corresponds to the days to come in the holiday, while Bet Hillel's reasons corresponds to the days which have passed. The other taught: Bet Shammai's reason corresponds to the descending order of the cattle sacrificed on Sukkot. Bet Hillel's reasons was that we ascend in the matters of holiness and do not descend.

One cannot use the Hanukkah lamp for personal needs. For that, one must have an additional lamp. If however, one has kindled a torch as a Hanukkah lamp, no additional lamp is required. If one has enough money for either lighting the Shabbat candles or to kindle the Hanukkah lamp, one should kindle the Shabbat lamp because it brings peace into a household. However, if one must choose between wine for Kiddush and oil for the Hanukkah lamp, one should kindle the Hanukkah lamp because it is more important to publicize the miracle.

In these passages we learn that the rabbis were indeed concerned about the affordability of oil to be used during Hanukkah, allowing for special provisions to enable a family to buy less oil. In addition, we learn of the rabbinic choice when a family must choose between kindling a hanukkiah and lighting Shabbat candles, or between drinking Shabbat wine versus the lighting of hanukkiah. Interestingly, with regard to the manner in which the candles are to be lit each of the eight days of Hanukkah, the ruling of Bet Hillel, which advocates adding an additional candle each day, has become normative.

Regarding the placement of the hanukkiah, we have the following passage from the Talmud:

One should place the Hanukkah lamp by the door of the house on the outside, within a handbreadth of the door, so that it is on the left side of a person entering the house, the mezuzah on the right side and the Hanukkah lamp on the left. If one resides in an upper story, the lamp should be placed in a window overlooking the

public domain. . . . In times of danger, one may place
the Hanukkah lamp inside the house, on the table. . . .
(*Talmud Shabbat* 21b)

Today, many people place an electric hanukkiah in a
window facing the street to comply with the rabbinic
injunction to "publicize the miracle." Maimonides wrote
in his Mishneh Torah, Laws of Hanukkah: "One should
carefully fulfill the obligation to light the Hanukkah
lights in order to publicize the miracle and to offer
additional praise and thanksgiving to God for the wonders which God did for us."

By the end of the first century, the basic outlines of the
Talmudic Hanukkah had been delineated. No new rituals and regulations evolved, and the festival apparently
remained confined mainly to Palestine. The emphasis
was clearly on the miracle of the oil rather than the
battles for religious freedom. The fact that Rabbi Judah
the Prince never included the origins of Hanukkah in
any part of the Mishneh is highly revealing. It is postu-
lated that Rabbi Judah the Prince, the compiler of the
Mishneh, was a descendant of King David. The miracle
of Hanukkah, on the other hand, came about through
the heroism of the Hasmonean dynasty, which was not
of Davidic lineage.

BIBLICAL ALLUSIONS TO HANUKKAH

Rabbinic thinkers have dwelt extensively upon biblical
allusions to the festival of Hanukkah. Their investiga-
tions have been based through the centuries on Hebrew

letter associations, gematriah (Jewish numerology), and the like. Following is a cross section of such allusions as recorded in Rabbinic literature:

1. In the Torah portion of Emor (*Leviticus* 21–24), the Torah mentions all the festivals of the year: Shabbat, Passover, Shavuot, Rosh Hashanah, Yom Kippur, and Sukkot. The section concludes: "Thus Moses declared to the children of Israel the set times of God." The very next verse (24:1) describes the religious obligation of maintaining an eternal light in the Temple with pure olive oil. The rabbis draw an inference based upon the juxtaposition of these ideas in which a Sukkah mitzvah is followed by the mitzvah of lighting the menorah with pure olive oil. The inference is that the Torah was anticipating a future time when the kindling of the menorah would become an annual festival, namely Hanukkah, which would directly follow Sukkot. (Sefer Rokeach)

2. In the Torah portion of Emor (*Leviticus* 24:4), we have the phrase "to cause the light to burn" followed by the next verse "he shall prepare the lights." The singular "ner" (light) followed by the plural "nerot" (lights) is asserted to allude to the practice on Hanukkah of first kindling one light, and on subsequent nights adding an additional light. (Sefer Rokeach)

3. At the end of every weekly Torah reading in the Torah, there is a Masoretic note in some Bibles which notes the exact amount of verses in that particular Torah portion. At the end of the portion of Miketz (*Genesis*

41–44), which is the portion that is almost always read on the Sabbath of Hanukkah, there is an additional note not found in any other Torah portion. It states that the Torah portion contains 2,025 words.

The Bnai Yisas'char asserts that the number 2,025 alludes to Hanukkah, which usually falls in the week of the Torah portion of Miketz. His reasoning is as follows: On Hanukkah, we light a new light for each of the eight nights. The numerical value of the letters of "ner" (light) is 250. Accordingly, the 8 lights of Hanukkah yield a total of 2,000 (250×8). Hanukkah always begins on the 25th of Kislev. Thus 2,025 is an allusion to the lights and the date of Hanukkah.

4. The twenty-fifth word of the Torah is "or" [light] (*Genesis* 1:3). This is an allusion to Hanukkah falling on the twenty-fifth of the Hebrew month of Kislev.

5. The twenty-fifth place of the Israelite's encampment in the desert was called "Chashmonah" (*Numbers* 33:29). This is very similar to the word "Hasmonean," the family that fought the battles that ultimately led to Hanukkah becoming its own unique festival.

6. An allusion in the Torah to the fact that we utilize the light of the shamash on Hanukkah is derived from a homiletical reading of *Genesis* 32:32: Instead of "vayeezrach lo hashemesh," "the sun shone for him," we read "vayeezrach lo hashamash," "the shamash illuminated for him." (Maharil)

CELEBRATING IN THE HOME AND IN THE SYNAGOGUE

IN THE SYNAGOGUE

Hanukkah is marked by the kindling of lights at home and in the synagogue. The candles are lit in the synagogue immediately before the maariv evening service. It is also customary to light candles in the synagogue before the shacharit morning service, but without the accompanying benedictions.

There are some variations to the liturgy during the festival of Hanukkah. For example, the paragraph "al hanissim" (for the miracles) is added during the Amidah prayer and in the Grace after the meals. Following is a translation of the al hanissim paragraph:

> We thank You for the heroism, for the triumphs, and for the miraculous deliverance of our ancestors in other days, and in our time.
>
> In the days of Mattathias son of Yochanan, the Hasmonean, the High Priest, and in the days of his sons, a

cruel power rose against Israel, demanding that they abandon Your Torah and violate Your mitzvot. You, in great mercy, stood by Your people in time of trouble. You defended them, vindicated them, and avenged their wrongs. You delivered the strong into the hands of the weak, the many into the hands of the few, the corrupt into the hands of the pure in heart, the guilty into the hands of the innocent. You delivered the arrogant into the hands of those who were faithful to Your Torah. You have wrought great victories and miraculous deliverance for Your people Israel to this day, revealing Your glory and Your holiness to the world. Then Your children came into Your shrine, cleansed Your Temple, purified Your sanctuary, and kindled lights in Your sacred courts. They set aside these eight days as a season for giving thanks and reciting praises to You.

The Tachanun supplicatory prayers are omitted during the festival of Hanukkah. The complete Hallel (*Psalms* 113–118) are recited each morning during the festival.

The Torah is read every morning and three people are called to the reading during the week. The reading is from the Torah portion of Naso (*Numbers* 7), and is known as "parashat nisiim" because it tells of the identical gifts of the princes of Israel brought at the dedication of the Tabernacle in the wildness. The presentation of the gifts took place at the time when Moses, after having completed the erection of the Tabernacle, anointed and sanctified it as well as the Altar and all the vessels connected with it. The offering consisted of gifts for the transport of the Tabernacle and golden and silver vessels for the service of the Sanctuary, with sacrificial animals for the dedication ceremony. The gifts were offered on twelve separate days. The narrative, describing each in unaltered language, reflects the stately solemnity that marked the repetition of the same ceremony day by day. None of the princes wished to outdo the other, but harmony reigned among them.

Here is an excerpt of the reading for the second day of Hanukkah:

> On the second day Nethanel the son of Zuar, prince of Issachar, did offer. He presented for his offering one silver dish, the weight thereof was a hundred and thirty shekels, one silver basin of seventy shekels, after the shekel of the sanctuary. Both of them full of fine mingled flour with oil for a meal offering. One golden pan of ten shekels, full of incense. One young bullock, one ram, one he-lamb of the first year, for a burnt offering. One male of the goats for a sin offering, and for the sacrifice of peace offerings, two oxen, five rams, five he goats, five he lambs of the first year.

On the sixth day of Hanukkah, which is always Rosh Hodesh Tevet (the new Hebrew month of Tevet), two Torah scrolls are taken from the Ark. In the first Torah scroll, we read the portion prescribed for Rosh Hodesh (*Numbers* 23:1–5) dealing with new moon offerings. In the second Torah scroll, we read the prescribed portion for Hanukkah, beginning "beyom hashishi" ("on the sixth day").

On the Sabbath, two Torah scrolls are taken out. The sidrah of the week is read from the first Torah scroll. The maftir, which is the prescribed reading for that day of Hanukkah, is read from the second.

Historically, because of the pride engendered by the Maccabean defeat of the Syrian-Greeks, celebrations of Hanukkah focused on the military victory. In response to this, the rabbis emphasized that the victory was only possible because the Maccabean freedom fighters were motivated by religious faith. To drive this home, they selected as the Haftarah for the Sabbath of Hanukkah a reading from the prophet Zechariah (2:14–4:4). It was chosen because it mentions the menorah and also because it contains the noteworthy verse "not by might, nor by power, but by My spirit says the Lord of Hosts." These words may be said to proclaim the lesson of all of Jewish history, and they are certainly the prophetic teaching of the festival of Hanukkah.

Since Hanukkah lasts eight days, it will have two Sabbaths if the first day of the festival is a Sabbath. In such a case, we follow the same procedure on the second Sabbath as on the first, except that the Haftarah is from *I Kings* 7:40–50. This passage has a description of the furnishings of the Temple of Solomon, an appropriate reading on a holiday that celebrates the rededication of the Second Temple.

If Rosh Hodesh and the Sabbath coincide, then three Torah scrolls are removed from the Ark. The sidrah of the week is read from the first, and six people are given aliyot. The passage for Rosh Hodesh (*Numbers* 28:9–15) is read from the second scroll for the seventh aliyah. The prescribed reading for the sixth day of Hanukkah is then read from the third Torah scroll, and the Haftarah is that of Hanukkah (i.e., *Zechariah* 2, 14–4:7).

IN THE HOME

Hanukkah begins on the eve of the twenty-fifth of Kislev and lasts eight days. Work is permitted during the eight days, but all signs of sadness are to be avoided. There is no fasting, and at traditional funerals, even eulogies are often omitted.

Light is a symbol associated with nearly all Jewish holy days and festivals. The Hanukkah lights mark each day of the festival and are constant reminders of the menorah which burned in the ancient Temple. Hanukkah is marked by the kindling of lights at home. If oil is used for the Hanukkah lights, olive oil is most preferred. If candles are used, wax are preferred. The weight of rabbinic opinion opposes the use of an electric hanukkiah, although many people do place an electric one in their windows in order to publicize the miracle of the festival.

One light is kindled on the first night of Hanukkah and an additional light is added each succeeding night so that eight lights are kindled on the eighth night. The lights should be kindled after sundown. Three benedictions are recited before the kindling of the lights on the first night: "lehadlik ner shel Hanukkah," "she'asah nissim la'avoteinu," and the "shehechayanu." The first two benedictions are also recited on each of the seven subsequent nights.

The first candle is placed on the right side of the hanukkiah. The second candle (on the second night), is placed directly to the left of the place occupied by the first candle, and so on, always moving leftward. The kindling starts on the left and moves toward the right. Thus, the first candle to be lit each day is the candle added for that day.

In addition to the candles that are lit for each day, there is a special candle known as the shamash. The extra candle is necessary because the Hanukkah lights themselves are not to be used for kindling other lights. Thus, the servant candle, the shamash, is used to light the other candles and to provide illumination. It remains lit along with the others.

Basic Blessings

Here are the basic blessings for the festival of Hanukkah:

On lighting the Hanukkiah
(*on each night*)

ברוך אתה יהוה אלהינו מלך העולם, אשר קדשנו במצותיו
וצונו להדליק נר של חנכה.

Barukh atah adonai eloheinu melekh ha'olam asher kid'sha-nu b'mitzvotav v'tzivanu l'hadlik neir shel chanukkah.

Praised are You, Adonai our God, Sovereign of the Universe, who has made us holy by mitzvot and instructed us to light the Hanukkah candles.

(*on each night*)

ברוך אתה יהוה אלהינו מלך העולם, שעשה נסים לאבותינו
בימים ההם ובזמן הזה.

Barukh atah adonai eloheinu melekh ha'olam, she'asah nissim la'avoteinu bayamim haheim uvaz'man hazeh.

Praised are You, Adonai our God, Sovereign of the Universe, who performed miracles for our ancestors at this season in ancient days.

(*on first night only*)

ברוך אתה יהוה אלהינו מלך העולם, שהחינו וקימנו והגיענו לזמן הזה.

Barukh atah adonai eloheinu melekh ha'olam she-hecheyanu v'kiymanu v'higi'anu laz'man hazeh.

Praised are You, Adonai our God, Sovereign of the Universe, who has given us life, sustained us, and helped us to reach this moment.

Since no single day of Hanukkah is more important than any other, traditional hanukkiot are designed so that all of the lights are on the same level. Only the shamash may be higher. However, many contemporary hanukkiot have been made without regard to this custom.

Originally, the lights were kindled in the streets outside the house, supposedly because Antiochus had forced the people to have pagan altars in front of their homes. Having Hanukkah lights there obliterated the former profanation and allowed the miracle to be publicized. Later, the custom arose of hanging the hanukkiah on the entrance of the doorpost, opposite the mezuzah. In that way, the hanukkiah would be shielded from the elements.

Maimonides, the medieval philosopher, describes the precept of Hanukkah lights as "an exceedingly precious one, and one should be particularly careful to fulfil it. Even if one has no food to eat except what one receives from charity, one should beg, or sell some of his clothing, for the purchase of oil and lamps to light." Maimonides also states that if one has no more than a single "perutah" (coin) and needs wine for the Kiddush and oil to light the Hanukkah lamp, he should give preference to the purchase of oil for the Hanukkah lamp over the purchase of wine for Kiddush, since it serves as a memorial of the miracle of Hanukkah. (Mishneh Torah, Laws of Hanukkah 4:12–13)

After the lighting of the hanukkiah, many families sing Hanukkah songs. The hymn "Maoz Tzur" ("Rock of Ages") is perhaps the most popular of all Hanukkah songs. Its words allude to the deliverance from Egypt, Babylonia, Persia, and Syria.

Many festive home customs are associated with Ha-nukkah. Game playing has been a part of Hanukkah custom for many centuries. It has been said to have originated during the Maccabean struggle as a means of subterfuge. After Torah study was disallowed, Jews would keep games on the table along with their holy books. The game of dreidel is a popular Hanukkah pastime. This is a spinning top game consisting of a metal, wooden, or plastic top on the four sides of which the Hebrew letters נגהש were engraved, presumably forming the initials of נם גדול היה שם (a great miracle happened there). Interestingly, the word גשנה is said to be borrowed from *Genesis* 46:28, read on the Sabbath of

Hanukkah, where we are told that Jacob sent Judah to Goshen. The numerical value of גשנה (358) is the same as that of משיח (messiah). The Israeli dreidel has the Hebrew letters נגהפ, standing for the Hebrew phrase "nes gadol haya po"—a great miracle happened here.

Since the miracle legend is associated with oil, various traditions developed regarding the eating of foods made with oil. In the Ashkenazic communities, potato pancakes (latkes) became the favorite. In many Sephardic families, jelly doughnuts (sufganiyot) fried in oil became the festival food of choice. These doughnuts are a popular treat today in the State of Israel during the Hanukkah festival.

Hanukkah has also become, especially for children, an occasion for the exchanging of gifts.

FAMILY HANUKKAH INNOVATIONS

In recent years, a variety of new family rituals and activities have been created in order to add an additional layer of meaning to the festival of Hanukkah. Here are some ideas that you may wish to introduce into your own family celebration:

1. **Have a Family Discussion:** Each night, have a family discussion about some aspect of Hanukkah. For example, on the first night you might want to ask family members to imagine what it might have been like to have been a Jew living in the time of King Antiochus and what way of life you may have wished to have chosen.

At another time, you might want to discuss the pros and cons of being a minority, and so forth.

2. **Volunteer to Help the Needy:** Volunteer to serve food in a local food pantry for the hungry. Enjoying one's religious freedom is a reminder that one must be proactive on behalf of others that are less fortunate. Working on behalf of the hungry and making food donations to the needy are ways of partnering with God.

3. **Affix a Mezuzah:** The Maccabees not only adorned the front of the Temple with crowns and shields, they also dedicated afresh the gates. Hanukkah is an ideal time to put a mezuzah in a room in your home where one is needed. The word "hanukkah" means dedication, and a mezuzah is a wonderful way of dedicating an additional room or space in your home to God. The mezuzah has also served as the distinctive mark of the Jewish home. The mezuzah consists of a small roll of parchment on which is written the Shema and the two biblical passages concerning the love for God and God's precepts (*Deuteronomy* 6:4–9; 11:13–21). Each time one leaves the area where the mezuzah hangs, one is reminded of the Jewishness of that space and one's commitment to Jewish values. Upon entering or leaving one's house, it is customary to touch the mezuzah with the fingers and then kiss the fingers. This is a way of showing one's love for God's precepts.

4. **Put up a Mizrach:** Mizrach literally means "east." By extension mizrach has come also to mean a decoration that is hung on the east wall of the house or

synagogue to indicate the direction of Jerusalem for correct orientation in prayer. The custom of turning toward the east while at prayer dates back to great antiquity. We are told that Daniel prayed to God three times a day and faced in the direction of Jerusalem (*Daniel* 6:10). According to the Talmud (Berachot 30a), the Jews in foreign lands turn in prayer towards the land of Israel, those in the land of Israel towards Jerusalem, those in Jerusalem towards the Temple, and those in the Temple towards the Holy of Holies. Hanukkah has become an ideal time to design a home mizrach and affix it to an eastern wall in one's home.

5. **Torch Run:** Some families have been known to plan a torch run around their block. Like a relay race, participants go once around the block each night with different runners, all lit by the shamash stationed in the front of the house. Try it, and invite your neighbors to participate too.

6. **Design Hanukkiot:** Many families, as a family project, design and produce their own family hanukkiah to be used during the festival of Hanukkah. See how creative you can be in designing your own special family hanukkiah.

7. **Gifts to the Poor:** In Eastern Europe, teachers as well as students often receive Hanukkah gelt (money). Among the Sephardim of Salonica, gifts of clothing and useful household items were traditionally given to new-lyweds at Hanukkah, whereas children received candy and money. Today, many families choose to buy gifts

and donate them to the needy. This is a wonderful way of sharing one's bounty with the less fortunate.

8. **Sponsor a Family Hanukkah Quiz Night:** Some families have an evening get-together with another family or two, and they play a question-and-answer game. This is followed by Hanukkah refreshments. Here are some sample questions and answers to get you started:

  i. How many blessings are said on the first night of Hanukkah? (Three)

  ii. How many candles are there in a box of Hanukkah candles? (44)

  iii. During which Hebrew month does Hanukkah begin? (Kislev)

  iv. What does the word "Hanukkah" literally mean? (Dedication)

  v. Who was Mattathias? (Father of Judah Maccabee.)

  vi. What is Modin? (The town where the war began.)

  vii. Who was Hannah? (A brave Jewish woman whose seven sons died for their religion.)

9. **Puzzles:** Jigsaw puzzles have been a popular amusement at Hanukkah time. If you do not have a suitable puzzle, you may wish to make your own. This can be done by taking a magazine picture or a photograph and gluing it onto a piece of cardboard. Cut the cardboard into a variety of pieces or shapes, and, lo and behold, you have a handmade puzzle ready to be put together by members of your family.

10. **Have a Zionist Hanukkah Celebration:** Here is a sample script for having a Zionist Hanukkah celebration in your home for the festival:

On this first night of Hanukkah, our candle reminds us that the Jewish People are One, and Israel is central to Jewish Life.

As in the days of the Maccabees, who we commemorate during this Hanukkah celebration, the Jewish people must unite in the common cause of making the land of Israel our national home.

On this second night we reflect on the miracle of aliyah and the rebirth of the State of Israel.

Traditionally Hanukkah recalls the miracle of the oil which burned for eight days and the rededication of the Temple. This year, let us also recall the miracle of a century of aliyah from east and west, and hasten the return of the Jewish people to our historic homeland.

On the third night, we reflect on Israel's commitment to building a society based on justice and peace.

The Maccabees went to war to fight against an oppressive ruler who wished to impose his will on the Jewish people. Israel was founded as a democracy, protecting the rights of all of its citizens to worship and live freely. This dedication to a vision of a just society strengthens and sustains Israel.

This fourth night we consider how fostering Jewish and Hebrew education and Jewish spiritual and cultural values help preserve our Jewish identity.

Antiochus sought to prevent the observance of Jewish religious practices, hoping that through this, he could eliminate Jewish identity. Zionism has been an important force in the preservation and strengthening of Jewish identity and values. Our commitment to Hebrew language and literature, and Israeli culture and society helps enrich our lives as Jews.

On this fifth night we recall Jews around the world who are not able to freely celebrate this Hanukkah with us nor live proudly and openly as Jews.

Just as throughout the millennia Jews have struggled to preserve their identity and culture, so too have others tried to take it from them. This Hanukkah let us redouble our efforts to protect the rights of our less fortunate brothers and sisters so that next year Jews everywhere can celebrate this occasion with us freely and proudly.

On this sixth night we give thanks that hundreds and thousands of Soviet and Ethiopian Jews have been given the opportunity to make aliyah.

The Jewish communities in the Soviet Union, Eastern Europe, and Ethiopia are among the oldest and largest in the diaspora. The chance for many of them to make aliyah and begin a new life in Israel is something for which Jews around the world have been hoping and praying for years, and for that we are grateful.

Our seventh candle is a blessing for the land of Israel.

We must always remember that there is but one earth, precious and fragile. A passage, nearly 2000 years old, best expresses our thoughts:

When the Holy Blessed One, created the first man, He took him and warned him about all the trees of the Garden of Eden, saying: See my works, how I created you. Beware lest you spoil and destroy My world, for if you will spoil it, there is no one to repair it after you. (Ecclesiastes *Rabbah 8,28)*

Our eighth and final candle is lit for shalom, peace.

Peace is in our hearts day after day, but we should take this season to rededicate ourselves to the hope of a true and lasting peace, not merely between Israeli and Arab, Jew and Gentile, but among all people of the world. (Prepared by the American Zionist Federation)

11. **Honor Someone or Something Special:** Some families choose to light each Hanukkah candle in honor of someone or something special. For example:

Candle 1: In honor of American soldiers stationed away from their families,
Candle 2: In honor of good health,
Candle 3: In honor of youngest family member,
Candle 4: In honor of oldest family member, and so forth.

12. **Make Hanukkah Foods:** Creating Hanukkah delicacies can be a wonderful opportunity for any family. Here are a couple of recipes to get you on your way:

Potato Latkes

3 large potatoes (2 cups grated)
1 small onion
2 eggs (egg whites for the cholesterol conscious)
2 tablespoons flour or matzah meal
1 teaspoon salt
Grate potatoes and place them in a bowl. Grate in the onion. Add eggs, flour, and salt. Drain off excess liquid. Drop by spoonfuls into well-oiled frying pan. Fry on both sides in hot oil. Serve with apple sauce or sour cream.

No Peel Latkes

1 egg
1 small onion cut into quarters
3 cups of unpeeled potatoes, cut into cubes
2 tablespoons flour
1 tablespoon oil
one-quarter teaspoon sugar
one-half teaspoon salt
one-eighth teaspoon pepper
Blend the egg and onion for a few seconds in a blender.
Add half the potatoes. Blend until smooth. Add the other
ingredients. Blend until smooth. Drop by spoonfuls into
a well-oiled frying pan. Drain on a paper towel. Serve
with apple sauce or sour cream.

Sufganiyot

three-quarter cup orange juice or water
one-quarter pound margarine
4 tablespoons sugar
2 packages dry yeast
3 cups flour
2 eggs, beaten
dash of salt
Combine orange juice, margarine, and sugar, and heat
until margarine melts. Cool to lukewarm and add yeast.
Stir until dissolved. Combine all ingredients and mix.
Knead until smooth (you may need to add more flour).
Place dough in greased bowl and cover. Let rise in a
warm spot for a half hour. Punch down. Shape small
pieces of dough into balls, rings, or twists. Cover and let
rise another half hour. Deep fry in hot oil. Put a few
teaspoons of powdered sugar or cinnamon in a paper
bag. Add doughnuts and shake.

13. **Have A Dedication Hanukkah Night:** Since the word Hanukkah means "dedication," some choose to dedicate the Hanukkah festival to a particular organization or cause and make mention of it after kindling the candles. In addition, their custom is to read aloud *Psalm* 30, the Psalm of the Dedication of the Temple. The Psalm is as follows:

The Psalm of the Dedication of the Temple

I extol you O God. You raised me up.
You did not permit enemies to rejoice over me.
God, I cried out and You healed me.
You saved me from the pit of death.
Sing to God, you faithful,
Acclaiming God's holiness.
God's anger lasts a moment
God's love is for a lifetime.
Tears may linger at night
But joy comes with the morning.
While at ease I once thought
Nothing can shake my security.
Favor me and I am a mountain of strength,
Hide Your face, God, and I am afraid.
To You, God, would I call,
Before God would I plead.
What profit is there if I am silenced.
What benefit if I go to my grave?
Will the dust praise You?
Will it proclaim Your faithfulness?
Hear me, God. Be gracious and be my help.
You turned my mourning into dancing
You changed my sackcloth into robes of joy
That I may sing your praise forever.
That I might thank You, God, forever.

BASIC HANUKKAH LAWS AND CUSTOMS

Following is a listing of the main Hanukkah customs and rituals as portrayed in the Code of Jewish Law (condensed version).

1. Every night, during the eight nights of Hanukkah, lights are lit toward evening in a conspicuous place to proclaim the miracle. These days are called Hanukkah, a hyphenated word meaning: they rested on the twenty-fifth ("hanu," they rested, on "ka," the twenty-fifth day, where כ and ה equal twenty-five in gematria.) from their enemies. Another reason for the celebration is to commemorate the dedication of the Temple, won back from the enemies who had polluted it. Therefore, some authorities hold that it is imperative to feast a little more lavishly during these days. Another reason for the celebration is that the work of the Tabernacle in the wilderness was completed during these days. On Hanukkah, every Jew should recount to his household the miracles

that were wrought for our father in those days. However, feasting alone cannot be considered a religious act, unless it is accompanied by songs and hymns. Charity, too, should be liberally dispensed on Hanukkah, for this is conducive to correct the flaws of our souls, especially when given to maintain poor scholars who are engaged in the study of the Torah.

2. No fasting is permitted on Hanukkah, but it is permitted to fast and to deliver a funeral oration on the day preceding Hanukkah and the day after Hanukkah.

3. It is permissible to do all kinds of work during the eight days of Hanukkah. But women customarily refrain from work while the Hanukkah lights are burning, and we should not permit them to disregard this custom. The reason the women have assumed this restraint is that the evil decrees affected them most. For the oppressor had decreed that a maiden before her marriage must first cohabit with the governor. Another reason for this is that the miracle of deliverance was wrought through a woman. The daughter of Jochanan the High Priest was a very beautiful woman, and the cruel king requested her to be with him. She acceded to his request and she prepared for him dishes of cheese, which made him thirsty. He then drank wine, became intoxicated, and fell asleep, whereupon she cut off his head and brought it to Jerusalem. Finding that the king was dead, his followers became panicky and fled. Therefore, it is customary to eat dairy dishes on Hanukkah, commemorative of the miracle wrought by means of a milk product.

4. While all kinds of oil are valid for the Hanukkah lights, olive oil is the most preferred, for the miracle in the Temple was also wrought with olive oil. If this cannot be obtained, one may choose any other oil which gives a clear and bright flame, or wax candles may be used, as their light also is clear. One should not inter-twine two candles, for that would be akin to a torch. The candles should not be made of wax that has been used in a place of worship for heathens, for that makes it odious. All kinds of wicks are valid for the use of Hanukkah lights, but the most preferred are ones made of cotton. It is not necessary to take new wicks every night. One may light the same wicks until they are used up.

5. If one lights the Hanukkah candles in a candlestick made of clay, it is already considered as old, and it may not be used again because it has become repulsive. Therefore, one should endeavor to procure a fine metal candlestick, and if one can afford it, a silver candlestick, in order that the precept may be performed in a grand manner.

6. It is a prevailing custom among the scrupulously devout in our land for each member of the family to light Hanukkah candles, one candle on the first evening, two candles on the second, adding one candle each evening until the eighth day, when all eight candles are lit. Care should be taken that each places his candles in a separate place so that one can tell how many candles are to be lit that evening. The candles should not be lit in a

place where candles are usually lit the rest of the year in order that it be discernible that they are Hanukkah lights.

7. The Hanukkah lights should be lit in the doorway that leads to a public thoroughfare in order to proclaim the miracle. Thus, it was done in mishnaic and talmudic days. Nowadays, since we live among other nations, the candles are lit in the house, and if there is a window facing the public place, the candles should be lit there. If not, they should be lit near the door. They must be placed within a handbreadth near the left side of the door so that the mezuzah be on the right and the Hanukkah lights on the left, and thus we find ourselves flanked by religious objects. It is preferable to place the lights within the door space.

8. The Hanukkah candles must be placed higher than three handbreadths (twelve inches) above the ground and lower than ten handbreadths (forty inches). If, however, they are placed higher than ten handbreadths above the ground, the obligation is, nevertheless, fulfilled. But if they are placed higher than twenty cubits (thirty feet) from the ground, the obligation is not fulfilled for the eye cannot well perceive things placed higher than twenty cubits above the ground. One who dwells in an upper story may place the lights in the window even if it is higher than ten handbreadths from the floor. If the window is higher than twenty cubits from the ground, so that the passersby are unable to see the lights, then it is best to place them near the door.

9. The lights should be placed in an even row. One light should not be higher than the other. There should

be sufficient space between the lights so that the flames may not merge and resemble a torch. Wax candles have to be spaced for the additional reason—they might melt one another by the heat and get spoiled. If we fill a dish with oil and put wicks around it, then, if we put a perforated cover on it, each wick is considered as a separate candle; but, without a cover, it does not even qualify as one single candle because it is like a torch. A candlestick having two or more branches should not be lit by two persons even on the first evening, as it would not be discernible how many candles it represents.

10. The time to light the Hanukkah lamp is immediately after the stars come out, and one should not put it off. It is forbidden to do anything, even to study the Torah, before lighting the Hanukkah lamp, but the maariv prayer should be said before lighting it. One should assemble the entire household for the lighting of the candles in order to give it an air of solemnity. Candles for the Hanukkah lamp must be large enough to burn at least half an hour. If one has failed to light the lamp immediately upon the appearance of the stars, one may do so afterwards and say the benedictions as long as the members of his family are awake, but if they are already asleep and the rite can no longer be performed in a demonstrative manner, one should light the Hanukkah lamp without saying the benedictions. If one will have no time to light the Hanukkah lamp in the evening, one may light it after "half of the small mincha," that is, one and a quarter hours before the stars become visible; that is, according to the proportions of the day, consisting of twelve hours from sunrise to sunset; and

during the days of Hanukkah, if the day is only ten hours long, then "half of the small mincha" is only one hour and two and one-half minutes before the stars become visible, providing the candles are large enough to burn one half hour after the stars come out. If they do not burn that long, the obligation has not been fulfilled.

11. The order of lighting the candles is as follows: On the first evening, the candle to be lit is placed at the end of the Hanukkah lamp, facing our right hand. On the second evening, we add one towards the left; likewise on every succeeding evening, we add one towards the left. The added candle is lit first, then the lighting of the other candles proceeds towards the right.

12. On the first evening, the one who lights the Hanukkah lamp recites three benedictions: "lehadlik" (to light the Hanukkah lamp), "sheasah nissim" (who has wrought miracles), and "shehecheyanyu" (who has kept us in life). On the other evenings, the benediction shehecheyanu is not recited. After the benedictions are pronounced, the candle that has been added that evening is lit, and while lighting the rest of the candles, we recite Hanerot halalu (these candles). A convert to Judaism says: "who has wrought miracles for Israel" in the second benediction. If, however, he has said, "for our fathers," his obligation is fulfilled. An onen (a mourner before the interment), heaven forbid, should not light the Hanukkah lamp. Someone else should do it, and he should only respond Amen. But if there is no one else, then he should light the lamp without saying the benedictions.

13. It is an established rule that the act of lighting the Hanukkah lamp is what constitutes the precept. It is therefore necessary that when lighting the candles, they should be in their proper position and of the required size. Hence, if the candles are lower than three handbreadths above the ground when they are lit, or higher than twenty cubits, and they are properly placed later, they are of no avail. Likewise, if when lighting them they lack the required quantity of oil and thereafter more oil is added, they are of no avail. Also, if the candles were placed where a wind is blowing and were likely to be extinguished, the precept is not properly performed, and we must light them again, but without saying the benediction. If, however, they are put in the proper place and are accidentally extinguished, the precept is considered as having been properly performed. Nevertheless, it is customary to relight them. It is our custom to avoid lighting one candle with another, but they should be lit by the shamash (servile candle) or by some other candle.

14. It is forbidden to make use of any of the Hanukkah candles during the half hour that the lights must burn. Hence, we place the shamash near the Hanukkah candles so that in the event we do something near the candles we do so by the light of the shamash. The shamash should be placed a little higher than the other lights in order that it may be obvious that it is not one of the required number of candles.

15. The Hanukkah lamp is lit in the synagogue as a public proclamation of the miracle, and the benedictions

are uttered over them. The candles are placed near the southern wall and are lit between the mincha (afternoon) and maariv (evening) services. No one, however, is exempted from lighting the Hanukkah lamp by the one lit in the synagogue, but everyone must light them in his own house. A mourner should not light the Hanukkah lamp at the synagogue the first evening when the benediction shehecheyanu must be said, for a mourner is not allowed to utter this benediction in public but he may say this benediction in his house.

16. Women, too, are obligated to light Hanukkah candles, because they also were benefited by the miracle of Hanukkah. A woman may light the Hanukkah lamp and exempt the entire household. Even children who are old enough to be trained in the observance of precepts must light the Hanukkah candles. For a blind person, it is best, if he can, to contribute something towards the purchase of candles with another. If he has a wife, she lights the candles for him. If he has no wife and he lives by himself where he has none with whom to join in purchasing the candles, he should light them with the aid of another.

17. On Friday, the Hanukkah lamp must be lit before the Sabbath candles. The Hanukkah candles should be large enough to keep burning for no less than half an hour after the appearance of the stars, otherwise the benedictions pronounced over them are in vain. If the candles are placed near the door, something should be put between them and the door to prevent them from being extinguished when the door is being opened.

18. On Saturday night, the Hanukkah lamp should be lit after the Havdalah is recited. At the synagogue, it is lit before "veyitten lecha" (and may God give you) is said.

19. One who is out of town and knows that his wife lights the Hanukkah lamp at his house should light candles wherever he is without saying benedictions. If possible, he should hear someone else say the benedictions over candles, intend to be represented by the other, and respond Amen, after which he should light his own candles without saying the benedictions. But if his wife does not light the Hanukkah lamp at his house, likewise, guests in hotels are required to light the candles and say the benedictions, or else they should give the hotel-keeper a coin and acquire a share in the oil and the wick. The owner should add a little more oil than the required quantity for the share of the partners. They should, however, make every effort to light their own candles. One who is in the city but in somebody else's house should return to his home when the time comes for lighting the Hanukkah lamp and light it there.

20. The oil and the wicks that are left in the lamps after Hanukkah should be burnt, for since they had been set apart for the purpose of a precept, we are not allowed to derive any benefit from them unless we have specifically declared that we do not set apart what will be left after Hanukkah.

21. During the eight days of Hanukkah, we include Al HaNissim (for the miracles) in the Shemoneh Esreh. If we have inadvertently omitted it and have become

aware of the omission before pronouncing the Divine Name (Adonai) in the benediction hatov shimcha (whose name is good), we should then start with Al HaNissim, but if we have not become aware of the error until we have uttered the Divine Name, we conclude the benediction and we need not repeat the Shemoneh esreh.

22. During the eight days of Hanukkah, we recite the entire Hallel. We do not say "tachanun" (petition for Grace) nor "el erech appayim" (One who is long in suffering) nor "lamenatzeach" (for the chief musician), nor "tzidekattecha tzedek" (Your righteousness).

23. Each day of the Hanukkah, we call up three adult persons for the reading of the Torah, wherein is recorded the sacrifices brought by the princes contained in the Torah portion Naso (*Numbers* 6). On the first day, we read for the Kohen from "vayehi beyom kalot moshe" (and it came to pass when Moses had finally set up) until "Lachanukkat hamizbeach" (for the dedication of the altar). For the Levi, from "vayehi hammakriv bayyom harishon" (and he that offered his offering on the first day) until "meleah ketoret" (full of incense). For the Israelite, from "par echad" (one young bullock) until "ben amindav" (the son of Amminadav). On the second day, for the Kohen and the Levi, "bayyom hasheni" (on the second day). For the Israelite, "bayom hashelishi" (on the third day). Thus on each succeeding day, for the Kohen and the Levi, we read of the present day; for the Israelite, of the day that follows. On the eighth day, we read for the Kohen and Levi, "bayyom hashemini" (on the eighth day) and for the Israelite, we begin with

"bayyom hateshii" (the ninth day), completing the entire portion, and also a part of the portion of Behaalotecha (when you light) until "ken asah et hamenorah" (so he made the candlestick).

24. On the Sabbath that occurs during Hanukkah, two scrolls are taken from the Ark. In one, we read the portion of the week, and in the other, we read the maftir "the day of the nesiim," corresponding to the day of Hanukkah, and for the haftarah, we read (*Zechariah* 2:14): "Rani vesimechi" (sing and rejoice). If the New Moon of the month of Tevet occurs on a weekday, two scrolls are taken out. In one, we read for three persons the usual portion for Rosh Hodesh, and in the other scroll, we read for a fourth person "the day of nesiim," corresponding to the day of Hanukkah. For Rosh Hodesh is more frequent than Hanukkah, and it is an established principle of law that between the more frequent and the less frequent, the more frequent has priority. If by error the portion for Hanukkah is read first, then even if the reading has not yet begun, but the one who was called up has already said the benediction, the reading of his portion may be concluded, and for the rest who are called up, the portion of Rosh Hodesh is read. If the portion for Rosh Hodesh has been read as need be, but by error, also a fourth person has been called up to it, even if we become aware of the error immediately after the benediction, then if only one scroll has been taken out, no more should be read out of it. If, however, two scrolls have been taken out and there is apprehension that the Torah will be slighted by the worshipers, thinking that a defect has been discovered in it, a fifth

person is called, for whom we read the portion of Hanukkah in the second scroll. After this, the half kaddish is recited.

25. If the New Moon of Tevet occurs on a Sabbath, we take out three Torah scrolls. In the first, we read the Torah portion of the week for six persons. In the second, we read the portion of Rosh Hodesh for the seventh person, beginning with "uveyom hashabbat" (on the day of Sabbath). After this, half kaddish is recited. In the third scroll, we read for the maftir "the day of the nesiim," corresponding to the day of Hanukkah. And for the haftarah, we read "rani vesimechi" (sing and rejoice). The rule that the more frequent has precedence relates only where both are read, but in the case of the haftarah where only one is read, that of Rosh Hodesh is superseded by the one for Hanukkah to proclaim the miracle.

HANUKKAH SONGS

The celebration of all Jewish holidays is made complete with music. The first Hanukkah was celebrated by Judah and his men with "song and harps and lutes and cymbals" (*I Maccabees* 4:54). It is also likely that the Hallel Psalms of praise and *Psalm* 30 (the Psalm for the dedication of the Temple) were sung as well.

"MAOZ TZUR"

Perhaps the most popular Hanukkah hymn of all time is the "Maoz Tzur"—"Rock of Ages," traditionally sung after the kindling of the hanukkiah. It recounts the wonders of the exodus from Egypt and the deliverance from Babylonia, Persia, and Syria. It was composed by a thirteenth-century poet named Mordecai, whose name is revealed in the acrostic of the initial letters of the five stanzas of the song.

The traditional tune, bright and stirring, has been

61

regarded as traditional since the sixteenth century. It has been identified as an adaptation from an old German folksong widely used among the German Jews as early as 1450. It has been suggested that the author of "Maoz Tzur" may have been the Mordecai ben Isaac who wrote the well known Sabbath hymn "Mah Yafit."

The entire Maccabean struggle, as well as the traditional interpretation of Hanukkah, is summed up in the twenty-four Hebrew words of the fifth stanza: "Greeks gathered to attack me in the Hasmonean days. They demolished my towers, and polluted all the oils. From the last remaining flask a miracle was wrought for Israel. Men of wisdom decreed eight days for hymns of praise."

Here is the "Maoz Tzur" in Hebrew transliteration and in English translation:

Maoz tzur yeshuatee
Lecha na'eh leshabeach
Tikon beit tefillati
Vesham todah nezabeach
L'eit tachin matbe'ach
Az egmor beshir mizmor
Hanukkat hamizbe'ach

Ra'ot savah nafshi beyagon kochi kilah
Chayay mer'ru b'koshi besheebud malchut eglah
Uvaydo hagedolah hotzee et hasegula
Chayl Paroh vechol zaro
Yardu ke'even beemzulah

Devir kadsho heveeaynee
Vegam shal lo shakati
Uva nogays veheeglanee

Kee zarim avaditee
Vayayn ra'al masachtee
Keemat she'avartee
Keytz bavel zerubavel
Lekeytz shivim noshati

Kerot komat berosh beekash
Agagee ben hamdata
Veneeyeta lo lefach ulmokaysh
Ve'ga'avato neeshbata
Rosh yemeenee neesayta
Ve'oyayv shemo macheeta
Rov banav vekeenyanav
Al ha'eytz taleeta

Yevaneem neekbetzu alayai
Azai beemay hashmaneem
Ufartzu chomot meegdalai
Veteemu kol hashmaneem
Umeenotar kanakanim
Na'asah nes lashoshaneem
B'nai veena yemay shemonah
Kavu sheer urnaneem.

O mighty stronghold of my salvation, to praise You
        is a delight.
Restore my House of Prayer and there we will bring
        You a thanksgiving offering.
When you have utterly destroyed the blaspheming
        enemy
Then I shall complete with song and psalm the
        dedication of the altar.

My soul had been sated with troubles, my strength
        has been consumed with grief

They embittered my life with hardship during my
   subjection to the dominion of Egypt
But with God's great power God brought forth the
   treasured ones,
Pharaoh's army and all his offspring sank like a stone
   into the deep.

To His holy temple God brought me, but there too I
   found no peace,
And an oppressor came and exiled me because I had
   served strange gods and drunk benumbing wine
Scarcely had I departed at Babylon's end Zerubbabel
   came
At the end of seventy years I was saved.

To sever the towering cypress sought the Aggagite,
   son of Hammedatha
But it became a snare and stumbling block to him
   and his pride was ended
The head of the Benjamite You lifted, and the enemy,
   his name You did blot out
His numerous progeny You did hang on the gallows.

Greeks gathered to attack me in the Hasmonean days.
They demolished my towers, and polluted all the oils.
From the last remaining flask a miracle was wrought
   for Israel
Men of wisdom decreed eight days for hymns and
   praise.

"HANEROT HALLALU"

Another popular Hanukkah hymn that is recited following the kindling of the lights of the hanukkiah is

"Hanerot Hallalu"—"These Lights." The song was created by rabbinic scholars who lived shortly after the redaction of the Talmud (700 C.E.). The song praises God for the miraculous victory over the Syrian Greeks. The priestly leaders, the Hashmon family, lead the people to a military victory with the help of God. The song also echoes the Talmudic dictum (Shabbat 21b) that the hanukkiah cannot be used for one's personal needs:

> These lights we kindle to recall the miracles and the wonders and the deliverance and the battles that our ancestors accomplished in those days at this season through the hands of Your holy priests. And throughout all eight days of Hanukkah these lights are sanctified and we may not use them except to look upon them in order to thank and praise Your great name for Your miracle and for Your wonders and for Your deliverance.

"AL HANISSIM:
FOR THE MIRACLES YOU WROUGHT"

The "Al HaNissim" paragraph (we thank you for the miracles) recounts the story of Hanukkah and is recited in the Amidah prayer and in the Grace after meals throughout the festival of Hanukkah. The story of Hanukkah within the song is a condensed account of the Maccabean struggle. This text is already found in the ninth-century prayerbook of Rav Amram Gaon. The Al HaNissim hymn basically serves to remind us of the story of Hanukkah and the obligation to thank God as the redeemer of the Israelites:

We thank You for the heroism, for the triumphs, and for the miraculous deliverance of our ancestors in other days and in our time.

In the days of Mattathias son of Yochanan, the Hasmonean High Priest, and in the days of his sons, a cruel power rose against Your people Israel, demanding that they abandon Your Torah and violate Your mitzvot. You, in great mercy, stood by Your people in time of trouble. You defended them, vindicated them, and avenged their wrongs. You delivered the strong into the hands of the weak, the many into the hands of the few, the corrupt into the hands of the pure in heart, the guilty into the hands of the innocent. You delivered the arrogant into the hands of those who were faithful to Your Torah. You have wrought great victories and miraculous deliverance for Your people Israel to this day, revealing Your glory and Your holiness to all the world. Then Your children came into Your shrine, cleansed Your Temple, purified Your sanctuary, and kindled lights in Your sacred courts. They set aside these eight days as a season for giving thanks and reciting praises to You.

"MY DREIDEL"

Fanciful songs are also a part of the musical culture of the Hanukkah celebration. A popular song is one whose theme relates to the dreidel, the spinning top game played at Hanukkah. It is called "My Dreidel":

I have a little dreidel
I made it out of clay
And when it's dry and ready
Now dreidel I shall play.

(*Chorus*) O dreidel dreidel dreidel
I made it out of clay
O dreidel dreidel dreidel
Now dreidel I shall play

It has a lovely body
With legs so short and thin
And when it is all tired
It drops and then I win.

My dreidel's always playful
It loves to dance and spin
A happy game of dreidel
Come play now let's begin.

"MI YEMALEL"

Mi yemalel gevurot yisrael otan mi yimne
Hen bechol dor yakum hagibor goel ha'am
Shema bayamim haheym bazman hazeh
Makabee mosheeya u'fodeh
Uvyameynu kol am Yisrael
Yitached yakum l'higael

Who can retell
The things that befell us
Who can count them
In every age a hero or sage
Arose to our aid.
Hark! In days of yore in Israel's ancient land
Brave Maccabeus led the faithful band
But now all Israel must as one arise
Redeem itself through deed and sacrifice

"SEVIVON"

Sevivon sov sov sov
Hanukkah hu chag tov
Hanukkah hu chag tov
Sevivon sov sov sov
Chag simcha hu la'am
Nes gadol haya sham
Nes gadol haya sham
Chag simcha hu la'am

Little dreidel spin spin spin
Hanukkah is a day of joy
Great was the miracle that happened there
Spin little dreidel spin spin spin.

"ONCE UPON A TIME"
(SUNG TO "THOSE WERE THE DAYS")

Once upon a time we had a Temple
Where every Jew would go three times a year
There we worshipped God in our tradition
Till suddenly a tyrant did appear

(*Chorus*) Eight days of Hanukkah (2)
We celebrate the festival of lights
Those days in history
Still live for you and me
Let's keep the flame forever burning bright.

Then at Modin Mattathias told us
"Whoever is for God come join our band"

Led by Judah and his faithful brothers
We drove the tyrant from our holy land

(*Chorus*) Eight days of Hanukkah . . .

Then we came to dedicate the Temple
How their hearts were heavy with despair
Impurities and idols all around them
And just one jar of crude oil was there

(*Chorus*) Eight days of Hanukkah . . .

But with faith in God we cleaned the Temple
And kindled that small lamp with hope and love
Then the story had a happy ending
Eight days of blessed light came from above

(*Chorus*) Eight days of Hanukkah . . .

"HANUKKAH, HANUKKAH"

Hanukkah Hanukkah
Hag yafeh kol kach
Or chaviv misaviv
Gil la'yeled rach
Hanukkah Hanukkah
Sevivon sov sov
Sov sov sov sov sov sov
Ma na'im va tov.

Hanukkah Hanukkah is a merry holiday
Tops spin 'round, candles burn
Oh let us sing and dance.

"NOT BY MIGHT"

Lo bechayil velo b'koach
Ki im beruchi
Amar hashem Tzeva'ot

Not by might nor by power but by My spirit says the Lord
   of Hosts.
(Book of Zechariah)

"OH HANUKKAH"

Oh Hanukkah, O Hanukkah
Come light the menorah
Let's have a party
We'll all dance the hora
Gather round the table
We'll give you a treat.
Sevivon to play with,
Latkes to eat.
And while we are playing
The candles are burning low.
One for each night,
They shed a sweet light,
To remind us of days long ago.
One for each
They shed a sweet light
To remind us of days long ago.

"NER LI"

Ner li, ner li
Ner li dakik

BaHanukkah
Neri adlik
BaHanukkah
Neri ya'ir,
BaHanukkah
Shirim ashir
BaHanukkah
Neri Ya'ir
BaHanukkah
Shirim ashir

My candle, my candle
My little candle.
On Hanukkah
I will light my candle
On Hanukkah
My candle will glow,
On Hanukkah I will sing songs.
On Hanukkah my candle will glow.
On Hanukkah I will sing songs.

Hanukkah Oddities
and Curiosities

There are many unusual, interesting, and odd facts and features related to the festival of Hanukkah. Here are some lesser-known facts about the festival of lights.

1. **Pagan Origin of Hanukkah:** According to Dr. Julian Morgenstern of Hebrew Union College, in the back of Hanukkah there lies a pagan festival of either the autumn equinox or the winter solstice, both of which occasions were and still are marked in many parts of the world by the lighting of candles or fires.

2. **Nicanor Day:** A number of different Jewish holidays originated during the Hasmonean period. One, called Nicanor Day, celebrated Judah's victory over a General Nicanor.

3. **The Halley's Comet Hanukkah Connection:** Hanukkah is often called "Hag HaUrim"—the festival of lights. According to a recent astrological theory, Halley's

comet came very close to the earth's atmosphere during the time of the Hanukkah story in 165 B.C.E. The comet's tail could be seen as a wondrous great light in the sky and was likely seen by the Jews after the victory of the Maccabees. One theory has it that because of this great light in the sky, Hanukkah has come to be known as the festival of lights.

4. **The Thousand in a Cave:** During the war against the Syrians, many of the people hid in the numerous caves that abound in the mountains of Judea. Once, when the king's officers found out that large groups of Jews, about a thousand of them, were hiding in a certain huge cave, soldiers were sent up there to attack them. It was the Sabbath day. The officers called to the people in the cave: "Come out and bow down to the idols, as the King commanded you. In that way, you will be allowed to live. Otherwise you will die."

The people shouted from the cave: "No, we won't come out. And we won't take up arms and break the Sabbath. We would rather die instead." The Syrians then attacked and killed every one of the thousand Jews.

After this tragedy, Mattathias instructed his people that from then on, should they be attacked on the Sabbath day, they were permitted to defend themselves.

5. **Hanukkah—a Second Sukkot:** Since the festival of Sukkot (an eight-day major festival) could not be observed that year while the war was in progress, Hanukkah was meant to serve as a sort of "second Sukkot." During the rededication ceremonies of the Temples, the Jews marched around with palm branches in their hands—just as we do on Sukkot.

6. **No Hanukkah in 3031:** Strangely enough, in the year 3031, there will be no festival of Hanukkah. In 3032, there will be two Hanukkahs, one beginning in January and a second Hanukkah later that year in December.

7. **Stamps of Israel:** On the first official stamp of Israel, there appears Maccabean coins.

8. **Never on Tuesday:** The first day of Hanukkah can never occur on a Tuesday.

9. **Zot Hanukkah:** The technical name for the last and eighth day of Hanukkah is "zot Hanukkah" (this is Hanukkah), taken from the opening words of the Torah reading of that morning (*Numbers* 7:84).

10. **Judas Maccabeus:** A famous oratorio written by the great musical master Handel is entitled *Judas Maccabeus*, based on the life of Judah Maccabee. The Jews of England are credited for its great popularity.

11. **Antiochia:** The Greek name for Jerusalem was Antiochia, which of course bears a great similarity to the evil King Antiochus.

12. **Hanukkah Rhyming Quiz:**

    i. What is Hanukkah gelt? (Dandy candy)

    ii. What is the word for a wrecker of light? (Candle vandal)

    iii. What is a term for a Hanukkah candle? (Bright light)

13. **Effigies in Kurdistan:** The Jewish children of Kurdistan have the custom of making effigies of Antiochus, which they would carry around asking for Hanukkah gelt money. At the end of the day, the dolls would be ignited to the cries of "Antiochus, Antiochus."

14. **Candles in Turkey:** It was the custom in Turkey to make the candles from the flax fibers used to wrap the etrog. From the remains of the Hanukkah candles, another candle was made which was used to search for leavened bread at Passover. These customs provide a beautiful continuity to the holidays.

15. **Lights:** Josephus, the famous ancient historian, whose history of Hanukkah is based on *I Maccabees*, does not mention the term Hanukkah, and concludes: "From that time onward unto this day we celebrate the festival, calling it 'Lights.'" (*Antiquities* 12:235)

16. **Psalm 30:** Sephardic Jews often recite *Psalm* 30 after the kindling of the hanukkiah. According to tradition, *Psalm* 30 was the Psalm that was recited at the dedication of the Temple.

17. **Hanukkiot and Pointed Stars:** Archaeological discoveries related to Hanukkah have included that of a hanukkiah that was a circular lamp in the shape of a pointed star.

18. **Where to Get Pure Olive Oil:** According to the Talmud, the place where pure olive oil was available for

the Temple was an eight-day round trip from Jerusalem (Meiri, Shabbat 21b).

19. **Jews Rested on the 25th of Kislev:** According to some rabbinic commentators, the name Hanukkah was given in commemoration of the historical fact that the Jewish fighters rested ("chanu") from their battles against the Syrian Greeks on the twenty-fifth כה = 25 of Kislev.

20. **Maccabee and its Etymology:** Some commentators explain the term Maccabee as being composed of the initial letters of the Hebrew verse in *Exodus* 15:1 "**m**i **k**amocha **b**'elim **'A**donai"—who is like You among the heavenly powers. Tradition has it that this phrase was emblazoned on the shields of the Maccabee fighters.

21. **Longest Grace after Meals:** The longest Grace after the meal is recited during the year when the new Hebrew month of Tevet (the sixth or seventh day of Hanukkah) falls on the Sabbath. When this occurs, three passages are added to the regular grace after meals: "al hanissim" for Hanukkah, "retzei v'hachalitzeinu" for the Sabbath and "yaaleh veyavo" for Rosh Hodesh.

22. **Seven Hanukkahs:** How many Hanukkah events celebrated by "dedications" are there? The midrash (Pesikta Rabbati 2:2) lists seven:

    i. The hanukkah (dedication) of heaven and earth (*Genesis* 2:1), which was commemorated by the setting of the two great luminaries in the heavens to light up the earth,

ii. The hanukkah of the Tabernacle celebrated by the tribal princes (*Numbers* 7),

iii. The hanukkah of the First Temple (*I Kings* 8),

iv. The hanukkah of the city wall (*Nehemiah* 12:27),

v. The hanukkah of the Second Temple (*Ezra* 6:17),

vi. The hanukkah of the Hasmonean Kohanim, the one for which we kindle the menorah, and

vii. The hanukkah of the world to come (*Zephaniah* 1:12).

23. **Hanukkah and Jewish Warriors:** The Hebrew word "chen" denotes grace. Thus, according to Noam Elimelech, the name Hanukkah could be meant to allude that the Jewish warriors found divine grace on the 25th of Kislev.

24. **Hanukkah Light and Talmud Scholars:** The Talmud (Shabbat 23b) teaches that one who scrupulously observes the kindling of the Hanukkah light will have children who are Torah scholars.

25. **Women, Leisure Time, and Hanukkah Lights:** The Code of Jewish Law (Orach Chayim 67) states that because of their important role in the Hanukkah victory, women should abide by the custom of not doing work as long as the candles burn, and they should not be lenient in the matter. (Some women have been known to put their Hanukkah candles in the freezer so that they will burn longer!)

26. **The Dreidel and the Crime of Studying Torah:**
According to folk tradition, the dreidel and similar games
were devised in ancient times by Jews who were impris-
oned for the crime of studying Torah. These prisoners
would congregate in their jails under the guise of playing
games, but in reality they carried on their Torah study
discussions.

27. **Hanukkah as a Class Struggle:** The story of
Hanukkah may be viewed as a class struggle, with
merely religious persecution as a toll of working-class
oppression. The Hellenistic Jewish aristocracy, in collu-
sion with the Syrian ruling class, exploited the Jewish
masses to fund the imperial ambitions of the Seleucids as
well as the excesses of the Hellenist cult. Ironically, the
religious persecution that was used as a tool to suppress
dissent became the spark that ignited the revolt.

28. **Maccabiah:** The international sporting games,
recognized by the International Olympic Committee and
held every four years in the State of Israel, are called the
Maccabiah Games, after the Maccabees.

29. **Eight Spears That Were Used as Hanukkah
Wicks:** According to the legend from the Pesikta Rabbati, at the time the sons of the Hasmoneans triumphed
over the kingdom of Greece, they entered the Temple
and found there eight spears of iron which they grooved
out, poured in oil, and kindled wicks.

30. **A Hanukkah Wordplay:** Three important words
related to Hanukkah all share the same three Hebrew

letters—shin, mem, and nun. Oil=shemen, eight=
shemonah, and Hasmoneans=Hashmonim.

31. **Judah the Hammer:** Judah was called "Maccabee." The Hebrew word "makkev" means hammer, a
possible reference to the strength of Judah the soldier.
This is why he is sometimes known as Judah the
Hammer.

32. **Coins and the Story of Hanukkah:** The First
Book of Maccabees records that independence was
brought to Judea. King Antiochus declared to Simon: "I
turn over to you the right to make your own stamp for
coinage for your country" (*I Maccabees* 15:6). The
Judeans now had the freedom to mint their own coins
and thus the first Jewish coins in history were issued as
a result of Jewish independence.

33. **Hanukkah Gelt:** In 1958, the Bank of Israel
initiated a program of striking commemorative coins for
use as Hanukkah gelt. The first Hanukkah coin portrayed exactly the same menorah that had appeared on
the last Maccabean coins of Antigonus some 2,000 years
earlier. In 1976, the year of America's two hundredth
year of independence, the Hanukkah coin featured a
colonial American menorah.

34. **Goose—A Hanukkah Dish:** Chicken fat and the
fat of other fowl was needed to prepare some of the
favorite Hanukkah delicacies. Since goose was a fatty
fowl, it became traditional to serve it on Hanukkah
and to render its fat, which was then set aside and saved

until Passover. Some of the fat was used to prepare "gribenes"—the crisp, fried fat of a fowl served with latkes on Hanukkah.

35. **Playing Cards and Hanukkah:** The custom of playing cards began about 600 years ago when yeshivah students abandoned their studies to celebrate the holiday. One way in which the students expressed the joyous spirit of the holiday was to play games of chance. Rabbi Levi Yitzchak of Berdichev defended this practice, explaining that Jews played cards on Hanukkah nights to train themselves to stay up late, which would enable them to study Torah for longer hours throughout the year.

36. **The Syrian-Greeks in the Hanukkah Story:** The Greeks who dominated Palestine in the second century of the common era were known as the Syrian-Greeks. Alexander the Great, the Greek king who ruled Palestine, Syria, Egypt, and many nearby countries, died in the year 320 B.C.E. He left no sons to succeed him, and as a result his two leading generals, Ptolemy and Seleucus, began a struggle that lasted twenty years. Ptolemy ruled Egypt and Seleucus controlled Syria. Both vied for control of Palestine, the crossroads of the ancient world. Seleucus was the victor. In the second century of the common era, Seleucus and his Syrian-Greek army dominated Palestine, and it was against their domination that the Hasmoneans fled.

37. **The Book of the Maccabees—a Non-biblical Book:** It has often been asked why the Book of the

Maccabees is not part of the Bible. The Book of the Maccabees is a part of the Apocrypha, a group of fourteen books of the Septuagint (Greek translation of the Bible) which Judaism did not consider worthy of inclusion in the Bible canon. Protestants do not consider the Apocrypha part of the Bible, but Catholics accept eleven of the books.

38. **Giant Hanukkiot:** During the festival of Hanukkah, giant Hanukkiot, visible for great distances, are kindled in the State of Israel atop public buildings such as the Knesset Parliament Building in Jerusalem. Today, the Lubavticher Hassidim often choose to erect very large outdoor hanukkiot in various cities in the United States and Canada.

39. **A Marble Hanukkiah:** A marble Hanukkah lamp was discovered from medieval times inscribed with this verse from *Proverbs* 6:23: "For the commandment is a lamp and the teaching is light."

40. **How Many Ways to Spell Hanukkah:** The word Hanukkah has many different spellings in the English language. Here are some of them: Chanukah; Chanukkah; Hanuka; Hannukka; Hanuko; Hannuko; Hannukko.

41. **The Hillel and Bet Shammai Controversy:** The talmudic argument between the Bet Shammai and Bet Hillel schools concerning how to light the hanukkiah was also used to interpret the word Hanukkah. According to Bet Shammai, the lights were to be kindled in a descending order—that is, eight the first night, seven on

the second, and so on. The School of Hillel proposed the opposite. The final decision is recorded in the name itself:

ח	eight
נרות	candles
דהלכה	and the law is
כבית	according to the school of
הלל	Hillel.

42. **Hidden Meaning of Hasmonean:** Some scholars have discovered in the name Hasmonean those elements of Judaism which the Syrians attempted to forbid the Jews from celebrating. Thus, the word Hasmonean was interpreted as follows:

חדש	New Moon Celebration
שבת	Sabbath
מילה	Circumcision
נידה	Laws of Family Purity
ארוסה	Sanctity of the Betrothal
יחוד השם	Belief in the unity of God.

43. **Hanukkah, Only Once:** Interestingly, the word "hanukkah" is found only one single time in the Bible, when Ezra and Nehemiah dedicated the walls of Jerusalem: "They sought the Levites out of their places, to bring them to Jerusalem, to keep the dedication (Hanukkah) with gladness" (*Nehemiah* 12:27).

44. **No God in First Book of Maccabees:** Strangely enough, the words "God" and "Lord" are absent in the First Book of the Maccabees.

45. **Explanations for the Eight-Day Celebration of Hanukkah:** There are a variety of reasons related to the miracle of Hanukkah and the reason for the festival being held for eight days. Here are several of them:

   i. The discovery of one jar of pure oil marked with the High Priest's stamp was a miracle,

   ii. After the oil was emptied into the Temple menorah and the lamps burned all night, they were found the next morning still filled with oil,

   iii. The jar itself absorbed some of the oil so that there did not remain even sufficient oil for one day, and

   iv. After the Temple menorah was filled with the available oil, the one jar remained full as before.

46. **Hanukkah in Christianity:** Hanukkah has a reference in the Gospel of John: "It was the Feast of the dedication of the Temple at Jerusalem, and it was winter." (10:22)

47. **Maccabean Saints:** Abbot Aelfric, a tenth-century English theologian, included the history of Judah Maccabee in his book *Lives of the Saints*.

HANUKKAH IN TALMUD AND JEWISH LEGEND

This Talmudic passage describes a mother and her seven sons who died for the sanctification of God's Name. It is a condensed version of the story of Hannah and her seven sons, which appears in the Second Book of the Maccabees:

It is for Your sake that we are slain all day long, that we are thought of as sheep to be slaughtered. (*Psalms* 44:23) Rabbi Judah said that this verse refers to the woman and her seven sons. They brought the first son before the emperor and said to him, Serve the idol. He replied: It is written in the Law, I the Lord am your God. (*Exodus* 20:2) So they led him away and killed him. They then brought the second before the emperor and said to him, Serve the idol. He replied: It is written in the Torah, You shall have no other gods beside Me. (*Exodus* 20:3) So they led him away and killed him. They then brought the next son and said: Serve the idol. He replied: It is written in the Torah,

Whoever sacrifices to a god other than the Lord above shall be proscribed. (*Exodus* 22:19) So they led him away and killed him. They then brought the next before the emperor saying, Serve the idol. He replied: It is written in the Torah, You shall not bow down to them. (*Exodus* 20:5) So they led him away and killed him. They then brought another and said to him, Serve the idol. He replied: It is written in the Torah, Hear O Israel, the Lord is our God, the Lord is One. (*Deuteronomy* 6:4) So they led him away and killed him. They then brought the next and said to him, Serve the idol. He replied: It is written in the Torah, Know therefore this day and keep in mind that God alone is in heaven above and on earth below, and there is no other. (*Exodus* 4:39) So they led him away and killed him. They brought the next and said to him, Serve the idol. He replied: It is written in the Torah, You have affirmed this day that the Lord is your God. And the Lord has affirmed this day that you are, as God promised, God's treasured people. (*Exodus* 26:17–18) We have long ago sworn to the Holy Blessed One, that we will not exchange Him for any other god, and God also has sworn to us that God will not change us for any other people. The emperor then said: I will throw down my seal before you and you can stoop down and pick it up so that they will say of you that you have conformed to the desire of the king. He replied: Fie on you, Caesar. If your own honor is so important, how much more the honor of the Holy Blessed One. They were leading him away to kill him when his mother said: Give him to me that I may kiss him. She said to him: My son, go and say to your father

Abraham, You did bind one son to the altar, but I have bound seven altars. Then she also went up on a roof and threw herself down and was killed. A voice then came forth from heaven saying: A happy mother of children (*Psalms* 113:9) (Talmud Gittin 57b).

The following Talmudic passage reviews the procedure for leftover oil in a Hanukkah lamp:

Let our Master instruct us: If a Hanukkah lamp has some oil left over in it, what is to be done with the oil. In keeping with the tradition of the amoraim, our Masters taught: If a Hanukkah lamp has oil left over in it after the first day, one adds oil to the lamp and lights it on the second day. If oil is left over after the second day, one adds more oil to the lamp and lights it on the third day, and so on for the successive days. But if on the eighth day some oil is still left, one makes a fire of the oil and burns by itself. Why so? Because the oil was set aside for a religious purpose, hence it is forbidden to make use of it for any other purpose (Pesikta Rabbati 3:1).

This Talmudic passage discusses the placement of the hanukkiah and the correct way to kindle the lights:

It is a religious precept to place the Hanukkah lamp by the door which is near the public domain, in such a manner that the mezuzah should be on the right hand and the Hanukkah lamp on the left, to fulfill what is stated, How fair are you, how beautiful (*Song of Songs* 7:7). How fair with the mezuzah and how

beautiful with the Hanukkah lamp. The number of
lights for each night is in accordance with the ruling of
the school of Hillel, [i.e., each night you add a light]
because in sacred matters one should proceed to a
higher grade but not descend to a lower one, and also
because the number of lights should correspond to the
days of the festival as they pass (Soferim 20:3).

This passage deals with the most preferable oil to be
used to kindle the Hanukkah lamp:

Rabbi Joshua said: All oils are fit for the Hanukkah
lamp, but olive oil is the best. Abaye observed: At first
Rabbah used to seek poppy seed oil, saying, The light
of this is more lasting. However, when he heard this
dictum of Rabbi Joshua ben Levi he was in favor of the
olive oil, saying, This yields a clearer light (Talmud
Shabbat 23a).

This Talmudic passage tells why the Hallel psalms are
to be recited on Hanukkah and not on the festival of
Purim:

Why is the Hallel read? Because one of the psalms
included in the Hallel states The Lord is God and has
given us light. (Psalms 118:27) Then why is Hallel not
read on Purim, when, as the Bible records, the right
was granted to the Jewish people to assemble and
fight for their lives. If any people or province attacks
them, they may destroy, massacre, and exterminate its
armed forces. (Esther 8:11) If the Hallel is read on
Hanukkah, why should it not also be read on Purim?

Because the Hallel is not read except on the over-throw of a kingdom, and since the kingdom of Ahasuerus continued, therefore the Hallel is not read. But as for the kingdom of Greece which the Holy Blessed One did destroy, the Jews proceeded to give voice to the Hallel, a hymn of praise saying: In times past we were servants to Pharaoh, servants to Greece. Now we are servants to the Holy Blessed One: O servants of God, give praise (*Psalms* 113:1) (Pesikta Rabbati 2:1).

This passage discusses the reason why the Hanukkah lights will shine forever:

Aaron was distinguished not only by being selected to dedicate the sanctuary through the lighting of the candles. God ordered Moses to communicate to his brother this revelation: "The sanctuary will on another occasion be dedicated by the lighting of candles, and then it will be done by the descendants, the Hasmoneans, for whom I will perform miracles and to whom I will grant grace. Hence there is greater glory destined for you than for all the other princes of the tribes, for their offerings to the sanctuary shall be employed only so long as it endures, but the lights of the Hanukkah festival will shine eternally (Or Zarua 1:139).

According to the Talmud, when the Hasmoneans entered the Temple after overpowering the Syrian Greeks, they reconsecrated it by removing the idols. They also found that the Greeks had contaminated all of the oils, and they found only one small flask of uncontaminated oil, enough to light the candles of the menorah for just one day. Here is the way in which the Talmud tells the story:

> Our rabbis have taught: On the twenty-fifth of the month of Kislev the days of Hanukkah begin. During these eight days the departed are not to be eulogized and no public fasts are to be declared. For when the Greeks entered the sanctuary of the Holy Temple they contaminated all of the oils. When the royal house of the Hasmoneans prevailed and was victorious, they searched but could find but only one single flask unopened and marked with the seal of the High Priest. It contained enough oil for just one day, but miraculously it burned for eight days. The following year they established these eight days as a permanent festival.

The following midrash presents us with an additional reason for why the candles are lit during the festival of Hanukkah:

> Why are lamps kindled during the festival of Hanukkah? At the time that the sons of the Hasmoneans triumphed and entered the Temple, they found there eight spits of iron that they set up and then kindled the wicks (Pesikta Rabbati 2:1).

In the Five Books of Moses, there is an allusion itself to the future miracle and to the festival of Hanukkah that would result from it. After the Bible concludes the portion concerning the part played by the Princes of the

Tribes in the consecration of the tabernacle, it is written, "And God spoke to Moses, saying, Speak to Aaron and say to him, Why do you light the candles" [*Numbers* 8:1–2]. The medieval commentator Rashi quotes from the Midrash:

> Why was the portion about the light of the menorah written immediately after the portion about the consecration of the tabernacle by the Princes? When Aaron witnessed the consecration of the tabernacle by the Princes, he felt discouraged because he did not share in it, not he himself, nor any member of his tribe.
>
> The Holy Blessed One said to him, "I swear by your life that your share is greater than this, for you shall trim and light the candles every evening and morning" (Rashi commentary on *Numbers* 8:1–2).

In the following Talmudic dialogue, we learn from the Talmud the preciousness of the commandment to light the Hanukkah menorah:

> Rava said: "It is obvious to me that if on Shabbat, a person only has enough money for either lights for one's home or for the Hanukkah lamp, one should spend one's money on lights for one's home, because they are necessary for domestic harmony. Similarly, if a person only has enough money for either lights for his home or wine for kiddush (blessing over wine), one should spend one's money on lights for one's home, because they are necessary for domestic harmony."
>
> Rava then asked, "If a person has enough money for

either the Hanukkah lamp or kiddush wine, which takes precedence? Does the wine rank higher because it is a commandment that comes regularly? Or does the Hanukkah lamp rank higher because it publicizes the miracle?"

After asking the question Rava found the solution: "The Hanukkah lamp ranks higher because it publicizes the miracle" (Talmud Shabbat 23b).

NOTABLE HANUKKAH QUOTATIONS

1. Not by might, nor by power, but by My spirit, says the Lord of Hosts (*Zechariah* 4:6).

2. On Hanukkah we are given part of the primordial light which has been hidden away since creation and is preserved for righteous people in the world to come. With this light, you can see from one end of the earth to the other. With this light, we are not allowed to kindle mundane lights but only other holy lights, the souls within each of us (Bnei Yissacher).

3. When Adam saw the day getting gradually shorter, he said: "Woe unto me, perhaps I have sinned, the world around me is being darkened and returning to its state of chaos and confusion. This then is the kind of death to which I have been sentenced from Heaven." So he began to keep an eight-day fast. But as he observed the winter equinox and noted the day getting increasingly longer, he said: "This is the world's course," and he set

forth to keep an eight-day holiday (Talmud Avodah Zarah 8a).

4. Rabbi Jose said: "I was long perplexed by this verse: 'And you shall grope at noonday as the blind gropes in darkness' [*Deuteronomy* 28:29]. Now what difference does it make to a blind person whether it is light or dark? Once I was walking on a pitch black night when I saw a blind person walking with a torch in his hands. I asked him: 'Why do you carry the torch?' He answered: 'As long as the torch is in my hand, people can see and assist me'" (Talmud Megillah 24b).

5. Furious they assailed us, but Your help availed us. And Your word broke their sword when our own strength failed us ("Maoz Tzur," hymn).

6. Who is like unto You, O God among the might? [*Exodus* 15:11]. (Note: These words were sung by Moses after he crossed the Red Sea. The letters מכבי spell "Maccabee" and are an acrostic for the phrase.)

7. Let us remember our ancestors, the Hasmoneans, who never put down their weapons nor gave up their faith. (Rabbi Shlomo Goren, chief Ashkenazic rabbi of Israel, made this statement when lighting the first wick of the oil-burning hanukkiah at the Eastern Wall in Jerusalem in 1974.)

HANUKKAH GAMES

1. DREIDEL

During the eight days of Hanukkah, everyone delights in spinning the dreidel. This simple four-sided top originated in medieval Germany, where it was popular with gamblers.

Purpose. To remind us of the Hanukkah miracle and the time when Jews played games during the medieval period.

Group. All ages.

Time. No set time limit.

Materials.
1. A four-sided spinning top (dreidel) with the following Hebrew letters on each of its four sides: נ (nun), ג (gimel), ה (heh), ש (shin). The letters are interpreted to

103

stand for the phrase *Nes gadol hayah sham* ("a great miracle happened there"). In Israel, dreidels are made with the letter פ (pay) replacing the shin; the substitution signifies that in Israel "a great miracle happened here" (*po*).

2. Nuts or candy used for betting.

Instructions.

1. Each player contributes an agreed-upon amount of nuts or candy, and then, spinning the dreidel in turn, pays the penalty or receives the prize indicated by the letter that is on the top when the dreidel falls. If the player spins nun, nothing happens and he passes; gimel, the player gets all that is in the kitty (in which case everybody contributes to make up a new kitty); heh, the player gets one-half of the kitty; shin, the player must put into the kitty whatever forfeit has been agreed upon when the game began.

2. The game ends when one player has won everything from the others or when all have had enough (the winner being the player who has won the most).

2. PIN THE CANDLES ON THE MENORAH

This game is a spinoff of the popular game that we all played as children called "Pin the Tail on the Donkey."

Purpose. Aside from the pure fun of attempting to append candles to a menorah when blindfolded, this game serves to reinforce the concept of the Hanukkah menorah having eight branches with a ninth candle (called the shamash) used to light the others.

Group. Ages 5 and up.

Time. 20–30 minutes.

Materials.
1. A 2 foot by 2 foot paper-cut menorah.
2. Cut-out paper candles 6 inches in length.
3. Cover the menorah with felt and attach a piece of felt to the back of each paper candle.

Instructions.

1. Divide the players into teams.
2. Give each player a candle.
3. Blindfold the first player. Give that player a paper candle and ask him to pin the candle on the extreme right-hand side of the menorah. Ask the next player on the other team to try to do the same.
4. The candle that is closest to the first wick on the right receives a point for the team.
5. Ask each person in turn to pin the candle on the menorah.
6. The team with the most points wins.

3. PLAY'S THE GAME

This game is suitable for play by more than one family. It is suggested that several families get together when playing this game.

Purpose. To allow players an opportunity to dramatize situations related to Hanukkah motifs.

Group. All ages.

Time. 45 minutes–1 hour.

Materials. A potpourri of household objects and four sacks to contain them.

Instructions.

1. Divide the players into teams. (Four teams are preferable, five players per team.)

2. Give each team a bag containing four items, along with the title sketch which it is required to dramatize.

3. Give each team 10–15 minutes to design its skit.

4. Call each team in turn to perform its skit. Inform the teams that they will be judged using these criteria: creativity, use of the items in the bag, and how well the skit relates to the festival of Hanukkah.

The following is a suggested scenario of one possible play of the game. The titles of the skits along with the accompanying items in the bag are listed below:

Sketch 1. "As the Dreidel Turns."
Articles. Empty wine bottle, large dreidel, flashlight, and umbrella.

Sketch 2. "Disco Latke."
Articles. Mop, funny slippers, toy musical instrument, potato.

Sketch 3. "Mattathias, Mattathias!"
Articles. Stuffed animal, aprons, shawl, funny hat.

Sketch 4. "I Can't Believe It Burned the Whole Eight Days."
Articles. Toilet brush, large candle, pail, cleanser.

4. THE MERRY FEAST GAME

The Merry Feast Game is a card game for the festival of Hanukkah. Since the fifteenth century many a long winter's evening has been passed in Jewish households playing various card games, so that playing this card game on Hanukkah would be keeping in the spirit of Jewish custom. This game is especially suitable for preadolescents.

Purpose. A game for pure enjoyment.

Group. Ages 10 and up.

Time. Several minutes per play.

Materials. Each of the four words of the sentence: "Hanukkah is a merry feast" ("a merry" is treated as one word) is written on a separate card. There must be as many cards as there are participants, but their number must be divisible by four.

Instructions.

1. Each player receives four cards that have the same word written on them—one player gets four cards on which the word "Hanukkah" is written, another gets four cards with the word "is" on them, and so forth.

2. Each player must exchange three cards with the others so that in the end he will be holding the complete sentence. The exchange may be done in one of the following ways:

a. Every player asks every other player for the card he needs. He will decide for himself whether the exchange he is offered is worthwhile or not and whether to hold on to a certain card or part with it.

b. Every player holds his cards spread out fanlike in such a way that the words on them are hidden from the others. A player who wants a card from another player asks the latter's permission to draw a card from those he is holding. As he cannot see the word on the card before he draws it, success is a matter of luck.

c. The player who first assembles the four words that make up the sentence wins the game.

5. DANCING DOUGHNUTS

This is a game for people who especially enjoy the culinary arts on the festival of Hanukkah. You ought to remember that in the United States the eating of potato pancakes fried in oil (latkes) is the custom. In Israel it is customary to eat fried doughnuts.

Purpose. A game for pure family enjoyment.

Group. Any ages.

Time. 20–25 minutes.

Materials.
1. String.
2. Doughnuts.

Instructions.

1. A piece of string is tied across the room at the approximate height of the players' heads. To that string, a number of short pieces of string are tied. To each of them is tied a doughnut which should reach down to the hips of the players.

2. Each player must eat the doughnut dangling before him without using his hands in the process. While the contestants wrestle with their doughnuts, someone will move the horizontal string slightly. The result will be clearly seen on the sugared faces of the participants when the game is over.

6. SCRAMBLED SENTENCES

Word games have been a popular amusement at Hanukkah time for several centuries. The following game involves the manipulation of words related to the festival of Hanukkah.

Purpose. To review the Hanukkah story through the manipulation of words to form semantically meaningful sentences.

Time. 30 minutes.

Materials.

1. Index cards (5 inches by 7 inches) with pieces of flannel affixed to the back.

2. One large piece of flannel covering the wall.

Instructions.

1. Place index cards with various words on them on the flannel board in random order.

2. Divide players into two teams and give them a designated amount of time to build a meaningful sentence related to the Hanukkah story, using the set of words affixed to the flannel board. For example, the words on the index cards might originally read: MIRACULOUSLY DAYS MENORAH FOR EIGHT THE BURNED." The sentence would be unscrambled to read: "THE MENORAH BURNED MIRACULOUSLY FOR EIGHT DAYS."

3. The team that correctly creates a meaningful sentence first receives the point. The team with the most points is the winner.

7. HANUKKAH SQUARES

One of the most popular current television quiz shows is "Hollywood Squares," which combines the popular game of tic-tac-toe with a question-and-answer game. This game is a spinoff of "Hollywood Squares" and must be played by several families.

Purpose. To review facts concerning the Hanukkah festival.

Group. Ages 10 and up.

Time. 30–45 minutes.

Materials.

1. Five cardboard menorahs size eight inches by 10 inches.

2. Five cardboard dreidels size eight inches by 10 inches.

3. Nine chairs set up in a tic-tac-toe grid.

4. Questions related to Hanukkah. (See sample.)

Instructions.

1. Choose nine players to sit on each of the nine chairs in the grid.

2. Divide the remaining players into two teams called the dreidels and the menorahs.

3. The goal of each team is to score a tic-tac-toe by deciding whether the players in the grid are giving true or false answers to questions posed to them. Every correct decision by team members is awarded the emblem of the team (i.e., either a dreidel or a menorah).

4. The first team to score a tic-tac-toe wins.

Sample Questions for Hanukkah Squares.

1. What does Hanukkah literally mean? (Dedication.)

2. Name a hero of the Hanukkah story. (Judah Maccabee.)

3. What do the Hebrew letters on an Israeli dreidel stand for? (*Nes gadol hayah po* ["A great miracle happened here"].)

4. On what day of what Hebrew month does Hanukkah always occur? (The 25th of Kislev.)

5. Name the Syrian king in the Hanukkah story. (Antiochus.)

6. Name a popular Hanukkah song written in the thirteenth century. ("*Ma'oz tzur*" ["Rock of Ages"].)

8. LET'S MAKE A MATCH

Purpose. An enjoyable and entertaining game of using one's imagination to complete sentences related to Hanukkah.

Group. Ages 8 and up.

Time. 15–30 minutes.

Materials. Written statements related to Hanukkah with the last word omitted are placed on index cards.

Instructions.

1. Choose three players from the group to be the "contestants." Divide the other players into two teams. These players are the "panelists."
2. Read a Hanukkah-related statement (see sample statements) to both the panelists and the contestants.
3. Each panelist is asked to write an answer to the fill-in-the-blank statement that will match the answer of the contestants. The contestants also write their answers on index cards.

4. Panelists reveal their answers, and the number of matches among the contestants is totaled, allowing 1 point for every match made.

5. A new statement is then read and the procedure continues as above. (You may choose to switch panelists after a given number of plays.)

6. The team with the most points wins.

Sample Let's Make a Match Sentences.

1. The technological age is upon us. As a matter of fact, by the year 2000 it is predicted that instead of spinning dreidels on Hanukkah Jews will be spinning _____.

2. Dora's latkes were so greasy that when you wrung them out you could just about _____.

3. Did you hear about the new improved five-sided dreidel? In addition to the letters nun, gimel, heh, and shin, there is now also a side that says _____.

4. Aunt Mollie was able to spin her dreidel for such a long time that by the time it came to a complete stop her friends _____.

5. A new recipe for latkes was recently invented by the Jews of South Africa. Instead of using potatoes, they use _____.

6. The new Judah Maccabee chocolate is now being made with nuts and _____.

7. Did you hear about the new Judah Maccabee doll? You wind it up and it _____ .

9. JEWISH IDENTITY HANUKKAH GAME

The following is a game idea for Hanukkah suggested by Dr. Dov Peretz Elkins in his book *Jewish Consciousness Raising*.

Purpose. To learn about one's Jewish identity by completing eight sentences regarding Jewish identity, one sentence for each branch of the Hanukkah menorah.

Group. Ages 10 and up.

Time. 45 minutes and up.

Materials. On a piece of oaktag is the heading: "Because I am a Jew . . ." Underneath are the following phrases:

> I appreciate . . .
> I demand . . .
> I wonder . . .
> I hope . . .
> I need . . .
> I should . . .
> I will never . . .
> I always . . .

Instructions.

Each family member in turn has an opportunity to react to each of the above phrases. In this way family members have an opportunity to learn how they feel about their Jewish identity.

HANUKKAH
IN THE SHORT STORY

HANUKKAH LIGHT IN WARSAW

by Stephen Fein

In the Warsaw Ghetto a fine, white snow covered the streets and lay in soft banks against buildings and gaping doorways. The late afternoon rays of the winter sun fell in pools of golden light on the darkening streets.

It was the Eve of Hanukkah. A young boy stood leaning against a splintered doorway. His hands were thrust deep into the pockets of his ragged coat. The boy stood motionless gazing absently down the empty street. Even the sharp gusts of wind that blew fitfully over the ghetto wall did not disturb the thin, silent figure.

A window was thrown open somewhere over his head and a woman's voice called softly.

"Jacob, you'll freeze down there. Come upstairs where it's warm."

Jacob was about to turn into the house when the sound of tramping feet caught his ear. Pressing close against the frame of the doorway, he stood watching.

From beyond the ghetto wall a group of men in military formation were marching home from their day's labor. They were Jews still strong enough to work. Their tramping feet came closer. One, two, three, four. One, two, three, four. Hemmed in by Nazi guards, they moved along like automatons, their faces blank, their eyes bleak and empty. One, two, three, four. Under their arms they carried small packages, food to keep them strong enough for the labor battalions. They were the only ones in the ghetto who were fed. Jacob could not tear his eyes from the packages under their arms.

The line of men shoved down the street. One of them seemed suddenly to notice Jacob. He fumbled with the package under his arm and a moment later something fell to the ground. Jacob stared. It was a turnip. The man glanced at him swiftly, winked, and continued marching with the rest of the group. One, two, three, four.

Breathless, Jacob stood waiting till they would disappear. A turnip! They had not eaten turnips for months, almost since the day the Germans had set foot in Warsaw. A smile lit up his face. His mother would not believe her eyes. A turnip would make a fine Hanukkah meal. When you were hungry, a turnip could taste better than pancakes.

The men turned a corner in the street and disappeared. Jacob stepped cautiously out of his doorway and looked up and down the street. No one was in sight. Only dark, broken windows and empty doorways. In one house, a candle burned. "A Hanukkah candle?" Jacob wondered. Where did Mrs. Grosz get a Hanukkah candle? She was all alone since her husband had been deported to Treblinka with his father. Perhaps she was lighting it for him, for her husband.

Jacob was about to dash out to the precious turnip when he heard the gay sound of boyish laughter. All about him windows were slammed shut. An old man ran down the street, wide-eyed, and disappeared into one of the houses.

"Jacob, come in quickly! They're coming!"

It was his mother again. Her voice was sharp and urgent.

Jacob turned and fled as two Germans, their faces round and their cheeks red, came gaily down the street. Jacob hid in the doorway and pulled the door shut behind him, leaving a crack open to see through.

The Nazis stopped in the middle of the street. A polished boot came down on the turnip, crushing it to pulp. They looked about them with laughing eyes. This was their "hunting" hour. Jacob saw them take their revolvers from their holsters and look up and down the street in search of prey. The eyes of one of them seemed fixed on Mrs. Grosz's candle. Suddenly his arm went up. He took careful aim and fired. A moment later there was a piercing scream, then the sound of a falling body. Poor Mrs. Grosz! Jacob could almost see her, a small, white-haired woman, sprawling on the floor under her Hanukkah candle. Still laughing, the soldiers returned their revolvers to their holsters and went chatting up the street and out of the ghetto.

Jacob felt his heart pounding against his ribs like a hammer. A cold sweat covered his body.

The grenade. Jacob suddenly saw the grenade his father had hidden so carefully behind a loose plank in the wall. "Use it well," his father had whispered when they were taking him away to Treblinka. "Use the grenade well, my son."

Jacob lay on his cot in the cold, dark room. In a bed a few yards away his mother slept. He could hear her heavy breathing and her restless movements. Sometimes she would start up in her sleep, calling him softly, and when his voice assured her that he was there, she fell back on her pillow.

Jacob listened to the ticking of the clock. Through the window he could see the gleam of the glass panes in the house across the street. The moon made strange figures on the wooden floor.

Jacob sat up. With quick, stealthy movements, he drew on his ragged clothes. Then he rose and crept silently across the room. A board creaked. He stood stock still, hoping his mother would not awake. She turned restlessly, moaned, but went on sleeping. Jacob's hand groped about in the dark till he found the loose plank in the wall near the door. His fingers closed around the cold steel of the grenade. Quickly, he thrust it into his pocket, then moved like a shadow to the door. The next moment he was walking down the stairs of the narrow hallway.

The street was deserted. A lean cat went slinking by, sniffing the cold snow. Keeping close to the houses, Jacob walked quickly to the Wall of the Ghetto. If the two sentries were there, he would hide behind the old oak tree, then, when their backs were turned, he would leap over the wall.

But there were no sentries at the gate. Perhaps they were in the tavern of the "Aryan" section of Warsaw.

"Just as well," Jacob murmured. "That's where we'll meet."

He leaped over the wall and quickly made his way to the tavern which the Nazi officers and soldiers used as a gathering place. The section around the tavern seemed deserted, too, like the streets of the ghetto. The Polish "Aryans" did not like the Germans any better than the Jews did.

The tavern was well lit. Sounds of boisterous laughter and singing reached out onto the street. Jacob crept close to the tavern and pressed his face against the window. Through clouds of smoke, he could see officers and young soldiers seated about small tables. A girl was sitting at a piano playing gay dance music which wound in and out between the heavy voices of the men. An officer stood leaning over her, a glass of wine in his hand. In one corner of the room, Jacob saw the two who had come "hunting" in the ghetto a few hours before.

Jacob stepped back from the window, his teeth clamped together like a vise. He saw the crushed turnip in the middle of the street under a polished boot. Again he heard Mrs. Grosz scream, and the thud of her body against the floor. For a moment he hesitated. Perhaps something would happen to him, and his mother would be left alone.

"Use it well, my son!"

Jacob ran back a few yards. He took the grenade from his pocket and carefully removed the pin. It seemed strange, he thought, that no one should be on guard. A shout of laughter rang out from the inn. Two glasses tinkled. Calmly, Jacob took careful aim, then flung the grenade. He turned and ran swiftly up the street. Behind him he heard a dull crash, the noise of shattered glass, the confused, frightened shouts of men. The piano tune ended abruptly. The whole street seemed to shake and heave.

Jacob did not dare look back until he had reached the safety of the ghetto wall. Then he turned around and gazed back. Flames rose from the tavern and licked hungrily into the dark night like a thousand greedy torches. "Use it well, my son." A smile lit up Jacob's pale face. For the first time in many months, he felt calm and happy. He had lit a Hanukkah candle for his father, for Mrs. Grosz, for every Jew in the Warsaw Ghetto. It was a Hanukkah candle the Nazis would not forget.

A MENORAH IN TEL AVIV

by YA'AKOV

"Hey, David! What are you dreaming about?"

David blinked and saw his two friends almost in front of him on the curb. Tel Aviv has some very busy streets, and he hadn't noticed his friends coming.

Joseph was still waiting for an answer. At last, David said, "About a menorah for Hanukkah."

What he did not tell the boys was that he was trying to think of a way to ask his father about a menorah. They had thrown out their old metal one when mother had been housecleaning before the summer. It had been bent and rusty, and the wax drippings from last year's colored candles were still stuck on it. He remembered his father saying, "By next Hanukkah I'll surely have a job and then we will buy a beautiful new menorah."

But only last night, when David was about to remind his father, the dog-eared record book with the family budget was open on the table. David saw his father

123

chewing the end of his pencil. He knew what that meant. There wasn't much work in the building trade these days. David swallowed his words and left the house.

Reuben broke in on his thoughts. "We were just talking about Hanukkah lamps, too," he said.

"Not just about any old menorah," Joseph corrected him. "Think of it, David, they are going to build a giant steel tower right here in the center of Tel Aviv. Maybe like the Eiffel Tower in Paris! And on top will be a mighty Hanukkah lamp. Each light will be a million candle-power! The papers said so today. All of Tel Aviv will be lit!"

David's face lit with sudden joy. "Really?" he cried. "If . . . if that's so. we won't have to light a menorah in our homes!"

Joseph roared, "You believe everything, don't you! Didn't you realize that I was just joking?"

"And even if they would build a giant-size Hanukkah lamp I would still want to light candles of my own," said Reuben. "You ought to see how beautiful our menorah is—it's all hammered silver, decorated with lions and birds, and the candle-holders are small and graceful."

"Our Hanukkah lamp uses oil," said Joseph. "You pour a little oil into each holder and light it. And then I ask my father to place the lamp on the window sill that faces the street, and I go down to the street and look up at our window."

David closed his eyes and said, "I think it would be wonderful to build a giant menorah. When I grow up and become an engineer I will build a huge tower in the center of Tel Aviv. I'll put a great menorah on top of it and each candle will shine with the power of a million candles and nobody will have to light his own menorah at home. On Hanukkah everyone will be amazed, because the night will be as bright as day."

"Say, I've got an idea," Reuben broke in. "Suppose we all go out on the first day of Hanukkah and look at the windows of all the homes to see who has the most beautiful menorah."

"Swell!" cried Joseph.

"Nothing could be more beautiful than a real giant menorah," David said, with a break in his voice.

Finally, he gave in. He could not tell his friends his troubles. Maybe there wouldn't even be a Hanukkah lamp at all in his house this year. And even if there would be one—it surely would not be made of hammered silver or burn pure olive oil.

Until the very day before Hanukkah, David had no chance to speak to his father about a menorah. His father had still not found any work. David nibbled his bread and cheese and wondered how to start the conversation. At last, after a small pile of green olive pits had accumulated on his father's plate, he suddenly said, "Dad, what do you think? Would it be possible to build a giant menorah at the top of a tower in the center of Tel Aviv, with a million candlepower for each light?"

"What for?" his father asked. "Where did you get such an idea?"

"If there would only be a menorah like that, everyone would be able to go outside and enjoy it. We wouldn't need our own menorah. Then those who could not afford a beautiful menorah of hammered silver would not be"—he finished bravely—"ashamed of their tin menorah."

The father studied his son's face for quite a while. Then he lowered his glance and poked with his fork at the pile of pits in his plate.

"A giant menorah," he said slowly. "No, David, there is no need for it. I understand your thoughts, my son. But the beauty of a menorah is in its small lights. They fill the whole house with a warm glow and they remind every single family of the wonderful Hanukkah story. Best of all is lighting them with your own hands so that you can see their little flames flicker."

"Father, tell me," David interrupted, "what kind of menorah will you buy?"

"Wait and see," answered his father with a steady voice.

David was on edge all day. He kept glancing at the clock on the dresser. When it began to grow dark and the Hanukkah lights started to flicker in the neighboring homes, David's father arose and said: "Bring a stout plank of wood, David, and nine potatoes from the pantry." Then he reached into his pocket and opened a penknife.

David soon returned with the board and potatoes.

"Take the knife," said his father, "and split each potato in half. In each half carve a hole big enough to set a candle into. We'll place the halves on the board and we will have a menorah."

David didn't know whether to laugh or cry. He took the knife and started to cut and carve. As he worked with the first potato, it seemed silly to him. With the second one, he tried to cut evenly and smoothly and with the third he enjoyed the idea. A potato menorah! Who ever heard of such a remarkable menorah!

The shammash candle stood firm in its holder.

The first candle stood upright too. And when his father started to sing *Ma-oz Tzur*, the two flames danced and so did their images in the windowpanes.

A few minutes later, David ran towards his friends in the street. Before they could say a word, he cried out: "What a menorah we've got! You never saw anything like it! It's made of potatoes and it's homemade and . . ."

"Potatoes?" asked Reuben. "I never heard of a potato menorah."

"Potatoes?" snickered Joseph. "What will you do with your menorah after Hanukkah? Eat it?" He burst into laughter.

David's spirits refused to be dampened.

"Look at the lights," he pointed to his window. In the back of the menorah he saw the blurry image of his father standing behind the lights.

"My father created that menorah," said David proudly. "It shines with a bright and wonderful light. To me, it's the most beautiful menorah in the whole world."

His voice trembled and his wide eyes glistened. Joseph and Reuben looked at him as though they were seeing him for the first time. Then they gazed long and hard at the potato menorah and at the shadow of David's father.

"You know," whispered Reuben, "when you think of it, it is a beautiful menorah."

And Joseph nodded his head in agreement.

THE GREAT HANUKKAH STRIKE

by Bami

Everything was topsy-turvy and the whole community was seething with excitement. The news was sensational, and no one talked about anything else. There was no doubt about it. It wasn't just a rumor.

The Hanukkah candles were going on strike.

That was their unanimous decision. Well—almost unanimous. Because one voice refused to join ranks with the others: the Shammash candle. The oil and the wicks and the tallow; the orange-tinted candles and the multicolored ones—all were firm. They would not burn this Hanukkah!

Here and there a few people were stunned into sadness. They knew they couldn't have a Hanukkah without lights. They even thought of declaring a three-day fast to mourn the terrible situation. Another handful of people, those who never bothered about Hanukkah at all, were, sad to say, quite pleased. "So the candles are

128

on strike?" they snickered. "Fine. We don't care. We'll be on strike with them."

But most of the people were just plain confused. It was a frightening thing to plan a fast for three whole days. But then, on the other hand, to join the candles in a strike? What would happen to the holiness and fun of Hanukkah? Cancel out Hanukkah? It would be the first time such a thing had happened in hundreds, no, thousands of years!

"It's an emergency!" cried some hotheads. "Let's make electric menorahs!"

"Never!" thundered all the others. "It must be candles or oil or no Hanukkah at all!"

The children were especially mixed up. They always had thought that Hanukkah was their holiday. It meant listening to the story of Judah Maccabee and eating potato pancakes and playing Hanukkah dreidel—and everything. Hopping up and down, the children kept asking the grown-ups: "Why? Why? Why? WHY? are the candles going on strike? There must be a reason. Please, tell us!"

Reason! As if those silly candles needed a reason. They seemed to have lost their heads. Thought of themselves as glorious suns, not simple little candles. Once they used to act their parts in a friendly, glowing way. When it was time, they would flicker without a fuss. Now their anger had flared forth and they flaunted their pride before the whole community. They had even written an editorial and placed it on the front pages of all the newspapers. What nerve! Anyway, here's what the editorial said:

"Kislev the 17th

"Little Hanukkah candles of the world, unite! In solemn assembly we decree a strike. We hereby inform everyone, big and small, fat and tall, that they will have to do without us this year.

"We admit that we feel sorry for all children everywhere. But it's the only way for us. What's the good of burning with all our might if hardly anyone cares? We try our best to remind you of the heroic struggle of our ancestors, the glorious Maccabees. But does everyone pay attention? Ha! Some don't sing Ma-oz Tzur, some think it's just a silly old custom, and some don't even know it's Hanukkah!

"Some light us only as an ornament, never seeing our inner flame, never realizing that we stand for victory over tyranny. We're not just tallow and wick. We have a soul. We stand for Jewish history!

"Well and therefore! The strike which we have proclaimed and decided upon unanimously—except for the Shammash—will go on until we have satisfaction.

"(Signed) The Hanukkah Candles"

The days rolled by and matters got worse. People had never given so much thought to plain everyday things like candles until this had come up. Hanukkah was fast approaching, and still no solution. The candles had become silent and refused to say a word. They all refused to do their duty, except the Shammash. The lowliest candle of them all, the one who didn't even have the right to stay on the same level with the other candles in the Menorah—he was the only one who wasn't going to strike. But what good would that do?

"Wait a minute!" someone cried. "Let's talk to him. Let's

go to the Shammash candle. We'll plead, we'll request, we'll do anything!"

So a small delegation, with serious faces, came to the Shammash. He received them courteously, nodding his wick in welcome.

"Listen to our plea," said the committee. "We are not worthy, perhaps. But think of our children. How will it be for them to grow up in a world without Hanukkah?"

And the Shammash promised. He would talk to his fellow candles. He couldn't promise anything, but he would try. The people were hopeful again, but nervous. It was just one day to Hanukkah.

The Shammash worked hard, and at last two-thirds of the striking candles relented. They would burn. But the rest of the candles were firm. The answer was no. They would not shed a drop of tallow for the cause.

Finally, the Shammash, weary with pleading, straightened up and said:

"I am the most humble among you. Each of you uses me to be lit up. True, I am your servant, but you can't get along without me. I am the only one who can go from one candle to another to light you. None of you may change places. You can't lower yourselves to light one another. I am lit on each of the eight days. I stay in my place and do my duty without question. Now then, I accuse you of trying to destroy the holy festival of Hanukkah. And, on my oath as a Shammash, I swear not to serve you this Hanukkah—or ever again. Unless you break up your strike, right now!"

The strike was over. Next day was a happy day in the world. Never had Hanukkah been celebrated with so much joy. In the fight for keeping alive Hanukkah, the

Shammash had fought like a true Maccabee and had won new glory. Tradition kept him from being placed on the same level as the other candles. True enough. But who said he couldn't be higher than all the rest?

That's where the people placed him. And today, the Shammash in many a menorah is placed a little higher than the others. From his position of honor he gladly descends to do his duty.

Then he climbs back up, and reminds the world that Hanukkah is a thrilling festival whose meaning we must never forget.

THE RESCUED MENORAH: AN AMERICAN TALE

Let me tell you about what happened last summer as I was driving crosstown on East 37th Street in New York City. I was coming from the airport where I had picked up my cousin from London. He was going to visit us for a few weeks. Exiting from the Midtown Tunnel and heading west, I was in the middle of the block, between Third Avenue and Lexington Avenue, when the light at the corner turned red. I stopped the car and waited. On my right was a garbage truck. The garbage man had just emptied a garbage can into the back of the truck. As I was conversing with my cousin, I noticed from the corner of my eye that the man then reached into the truck and pulled out a shiny metal object. I looked directly at what he was holding in his hands and saw that it was a brass Hanukkah *menorah*. My mind raced. Signalling to my cousin to roll down the window, I called out, "Sir, that object you are holding in your hand is a religious object that belongs in a Jewish place." The garbage man came closer to the car and said, "Someone has just thrown this out—probably belonged to some old person."

Again I said, trying not to sound too eager, though speaking hurriedly, "But it is a religious object that should be in a synagogue, perhaps. Would you give it to me so I can bring it to a synagogue or give it to someone who would use it at holiday time?"

He examined the *menorah*, as though weighing it in both his hands and mind, perhaps realizing that it might have some value—or that it might serve as a nice candle holder for his home.

The light changed. Horns were beginning to sound, so I felt I had to move on. What else could I say? Would there be enough time to explain the *mitzvah* of returning this *menorah* to its proper use? How much money could I offer so he would sell it to me? Should I pull in front of his truck and plead my case more strongly? In the quickness of the moment, I just couldn't think fast enough.

Suddenly in my mind's eye, with a rush of memory, I was standing in my Bubbe and Zaide's apartment and together we were celebrating Hanukkah.

My Bubbe and Zaide came from the old country. When I was a child I heard how they had come here to America, to a new country, a young country, and I decided they must have "thrown out" the old country, as if they had used it up or worn it out, like a neighbor who had thrown away the welcome mat because another neighbor had worn it out. We had a mat in front of our door with the word WELCOME on it, and it never seemed to wear out. But maybe ours cost more. It was all very puzzling for a little girl. Maybe my grandparents and the rest of their big family had to leave Russia because there was no more room for anyone else. Why else would people leave their home, the place where they grew up, where their friends were? It certainly was confusing to me. But at the time I didn't know the right questions to ask to better understand the immigration of the Jews and the reasons why they had left their old home. However, as I grew older I became better at asking questions. I asked, "What's an old country?" and "Which old country?" and "What did they do with the old country?" and "Could they make it new again?" I heard them talking about how a country has a soul, so I said they could make it new by repairing the "soles," like on a pair of shoes.

"What do children know about such things?" said my parents. "When you grow up, you'll understand more. You'll have *seichel* and then you'll ask," they would add patiently, smiling.

Wisdom must come automatically when you grow up, I reasoned. "But what age is grown-up?" I persisted.

They never could answer that question to my satisfaction. All they would tell me is, "You are grown-up when you have *seichel*!"

My Bubbe had a few things she had brought with her from her old home. She had several silver candlesticks, some gigantic feather quilts, and pillows stuffed with goose feathers that she and her mother had themselves plucked, and a *menorah* for Hanukkah. The *menorah* was made of brass. It looked like a tree composed of four pairs of open arms. I loved that *menorah*. Every Hanukkah, Bubbe would take it from the big glass cabinet, along with a smaller *menorah* for me, and place them on the table in front of the big window of her dining room, a room that faced the elevated railroad tracks on Park Avenue at the corner of 104th Street in New York City. Their third-floor apartment, called a railroad apartment, probably because it was long like a railroad car, was in a brownstone at 1401 Park Avenue. This was a section of the city called Harlem, and in the 1930s and 1940s, many Jews lived there. Whenever a train rumbled by, everyone felt the vibrations and heard the noise. While the Hanukkah candles were lit, the flames would dance even faster than usual, just for those few seconds. And when that happened, I would imagine to myself that it was Elijah walking by with his big cape flapping in the wind, causing the vibrations and checking to see if I had lit the candles and if I was watching them until they melted down and went out. Bubbe had always told me that it is a *mitzvah* to watch the candles once they are lit. "Remember," she would say in her Russian-Yiddish accent, "it is important to remember that watching the candles is part of the celebration of Hanukkah with all its miracles. The little flames add joy and light. They give us a message from thousands of years ago. They are saying that once there is light, you will never accept darkness again. So, my Malkele, do not leave the room while the candles are burning because otherwise, if you leave the room and leave the candles alone, you will shame them." That's how Bubbe spoke. Always with a lesson, always with a proverb, always with the faith and beliefs of the Jewish people. Bubbe could never have been a child like me, she was always a wise old woman, with plenty of *seichel*. I was sure of that.

What I also liked about being in Bubbe's house during Hanukkah were the *latkes* she made. "They are so delicious, Bubbe—even better than my mother's!" I would shout with a laugh, reaching for my tenth, or was it my twelfth *latke*?

"Sha, sha, my Malkele," my Bubbe would answer. "Your mama makes her *latkes* just like I do. She learned from me. But your mama is more modern than I am and knows how to cook better than me." But I would only smile and shake my head and hug my Bubbe tighter.

I also loved the stories Bubbe told. Whenever she was about to tell me a story, she would take off her flowered apron (my Bubbe loved roses so the apron had big roses all over it), sit in her favorite big cushioned chair near the *menorah*, and motion me to come sit next to her.

One Hanukkah, when I was very very young, Bubbe said, "I will tell you a story by Yehuda Leib Peretz, one of the great Yiddish writers." She explained that she had heard the story in the old country. I heard the story when I was young and this is how I remember it.

"Well, you see," she would start, "there was once a couple who lived happily together. They were poor, but happy. And when it came time for Hanukkah, they would take their brass Hanukkah lamp from its glass case and light the candles while they recited the blessings. That's how it was for years."

"What did the *menorah* look like, Bubbe?"

"Well, it had one twisted leg. There were brass birds in trees, and a big lion with its mouth open. Maybe it was laughing. On Hanukkah even a lion is happy," she would say with a laugh that made the wrinkles on her face even deeper. Then she would continue, "And Shloime-Zalmen, that was the husband's name, one day found some kind of iron in the street. When he arrived home, he cleaned the iron and underneath he saw that it was made of gold. So now he was a rich man. Well, they changed their name, they changed the way they dressed, they changed their address, and the children also changed schools to go to a fancy private school—no more *yeshivas*. They sold everything they owned and bought fancy French high-toned antiques. They even gave away their holy books. But the circle keeps turning, and after a few years, they were no longer so rich. Things went from bad to worse—no use going into detail—but they could no longer afford the things they had been used to. Meanwhile, their sons were in schools in another country, in England, far away.

"Now when this couple was poor again, they remembered that they were Jews. So Shloime-Zalmen went to *shul* again. And when it was time for Hanukkah, they remembered their old brass *menorah*. They searched everywhere for it hoping that maybe they hadn't thrown it away. In a corner near the stove, or maybe it was on top of the stove, they found it. Oh, they were so happy to see it, like a good old friend! They cleaned it and recited the blessings and lit the candles. They felt lighter in their hearts.

"One evening the doorbell rang and when they went to the door, standing there was an old furniture dealer they knew. 'Excuse me for disturbing you so late at night, but there is an Englishman who is an antique dealer and he is looking for old things to buy. Since I once bought old furniture from you, perhaps you still have some old things?' Standing behind the dealer was a man who looked like a *graf*, a nobleman. So Shloime-Zalmen invited them both in. As soon as the Englishman saw the Hanukkah *menorah*, he said he wanted to buy it. 'How much do you want for that brass object?' he asked. And Shloime-Zalmen didn't know what to answer.

"He looked at his wife. She gave him the answer, but only with her eyes and a slight shake of her head from side to side. But he knew what she meant. 'No, no, thank you. We cannot accept your offer because it is Hanukkah and we must light the candles each night. This is a *menorah* that we have had a long time. There must be a reason why we kept it, even when we didn't use if for a few years.'

"Soon after that night, things began to turn good again for this couple."

Many years have now gone by and my Bubbe and Zaide have died. I don't know what happened to my Bubbe's Hanukkah *menorah*—Bubbe's *menorah*! Suddenly I knew that the *menorah* rescued from the garbage truck had reminded me of my Bubbe's *menorah*.

The car horns were deafening. Going with my impulse, I pulled in front of the garbage truck, got out of my car—reaching into my pocketbook at the same time, took out a large bill, and handed it to the man holding the *menorah*, hoping he would sell it to me.

"No, no, lady. I couldn't take any money for it. I'm a religious man myself. This is a Jewish candlestick, is it? Then you take it and give it to someone who needs it

and will use it. Good luck, and God bless you, lady."
With a wave of his hand, he handed me the *menorah*
and jumped onto the back of the garbage truck, smiling
a great big smile.

Every year, that *menorah*—the *menorah* rescued on
37th Street—brings to my mind the *menorahs* of my
childhood, the one at Bubbe's house and the one in her
story. Did that discarded *menorah* really belong to an
old person? Then who would have thrown it away?
Maybe that person died and someone had come to clean
out the apartment.

Oh, perhaps you want to know what happened to that
menorah. I brought it to my rabbi and he gave it to a
young couple who had just arrived from Soviet Russia to
make a new life for themselves in America.

THE SECRET OF THE SHAMMASH:
A SEPHARDIC TALE

In the ancient city of Constantinople lived a Jewish doctor by the name of Nissim Rahamim. He was a scholar and a beloved physician well known to all for his wise and kind treatment of his patients.

When news of this doctor reached the ears of the Sultan, he began to ask many questions about Nissim. The Sultan was always asking questions, because he was so curious about everything in the world, and was surrounded by many wise men who knew many things. One day, the Sultan summoned Nissim Rahamim to come before him, and as they spoke, the Sultan became amazed at Nissim's wisdom and ways. At the conclusion of their meeting the Sultan appointed Nissim to be his personal physician. As time went by, Nissim and the Sultan became friends. Not only would Nissim visit the Sultan in the palace, but the Sultan would also visit Nissim at his home.

It so happened that on the last night of Hanukkah, the

Sultan came for a visit. When he entered the house, he saw the glow of the Hanukkah lamp and was filled with a happiness he had not felt before. He saw the whole family sitting around the table eating pancakes and playing with a spinning top. The doctor welcomed the guest and invited the Sultan to sit at the table with them, offering to teach him to play the game of *dreidle*. Immediately, the Sultan drew his chair closer and accepted the offer.

"You see that each of us has a pile of nuts that we use in place of coins. Each one takes a turn spinning the *dreidle*, which has a Hebrew letter engraved on each side. Each letter, *nun*, *gimmel*, *hey*, *shin*, stands for a Hebrew word. When the *dreidle* falls on the *nun*, nothing happens, and no one wins or loses any nuts. When it falls on *gimmel*, then that player wins all the nuts in the middle. *Hey* means that the player receives half the nuts. *Shin* means that the player loses and puts all his nuts into the middle.

The Sultan listened carefully and soon was playing easily and often the *dreidle* would fall on *gimmel*. "You say that the Hebrew letters stand for words. What words, Nissim?"

"They stand for '*Nes Gadol Haya Sham*,' which means 'A Great Miracle Happened There,'" answered Nissim.

"A miracle? What miracle?" asked the Sultan.

So Nissim told the Sultan about the Maccabees and why they fought and how they defeated the armies of Antiochus. Then he continued his narrative explaining how the Jews arrived at the Temple in Jerusalem and how they rededicated it with the holy oil.

"The miracle? It was all a miracle from God, but the

miracle of renewed hope and rededication, of a little pot of oil that continued to burn for eight days instead of for the expected one day, the miracle that this reminded us that we Jews are a light to the world, all of these are the miracle of Hanukkah," answered Nissim. "Since that time, we celebrate and remember to rededicate ourselves just as the Maccabees did in those times. Ah, but now it is your turn to spin the *dreidle*." And Nissim gave the Sultan the *dreidle* and the playing continued.

The Sultan looked carefully around the room in between his turns. He noticed the Hanukkah lamp, which stood on a table near the door. "Why do you place the lamp near the door? Why not in the center of the main table, here?" asked the Sultan.

Nissim explained, "The *hanukkiah*, as we call the Hanukkah lamp, is placed near the door so that it is near the *mezuzah*. Since it is a *mitzvah* to light the candles each of the nights of the festival, by placing the lamp near the door post, there is a *mitzvah* on both sides of the door."

They continued playing the game of *dreidle*, but the Sultan, curious about the many new things around him, asked, "And why do you have so many candles?"

And Nissim told him that there were eight days of the festival because the little cruse of oil lasted for eight days. "So we burn an additional candle for each night of the holiday until all eight candles are burning bright, just as you see here on this last night of Hanukkah."

But the Sultan raised his eyebrows and looked again at the *hanukkiah*, counting the candles. "But I see a ninth candle that is placed higher than the others. Why is that?"

"This candle is not counted as part of the eight. It is

called the *shammash*. It is the servant that is used to light the other candles. But we place it higher than the others. We are not permitted to use the light of the candles. So when we enjoy their light, we can say we enjoy the light of the *shammash*," answered Nissim.

But the Sultan was still not satisfied with this explanation. "I am certain that there is a hidden meaning to the *shammash* or else why would you keep it lighted, and why on a higher level? Perhaps there is a secret that you do not wish to tell me? That is known only between Jews?"

But before Nissim could deny this, the Sultan continued, "Come to the palace in three days' time and reveal the secret of the *shammash*." And with these words, the Sultan stood up, bid good night to the family, and left the house.

What was Nissim to do? What could he tell the Sultan about the "secret of the *shammash*," since there was no secret? He had read and studied all the works in the Talmud, and he had never heard of any secret. Should he make up something that might satisfy the Sultan? For the next two days, the doctor's thoughts were filled with this dilemma.

On the night of the second day Nissim decided to take a walk in the cool air. It was so quiet that he could hear the echo of his own footsteps. Suddenly an old man was walking beside him. Nissim had not heard him. He had not noticed him before. They walked for a while in silence. Then turning to Nissim, the old man said, "Well, Nissim, who will carry whom?"

Nissim looked at the old man curiously and wondered if he was crazy. I might be able to carry you, he thought, but you are much too old and frail to carry me. Nissim did not reply, thinking that perhaps he had not heard the man correctly.

After a while, they passed a house from which sounds of weeping could be heard. The coffin near the door told them this was a house of mourning. As they passed, the old man turned to Nissim and asked, "Do you think the man in the coffin is alive or dead?"

Now Nissim understood that the old man was confused and decided not to answer a madman.

As they continued on the walk, they passed a field where the wheat was ready for reaping. "What full ears of wheat! But I would like to know if it has already been eaten," said the old man.

Again Nissim did not know how to reply, and only shrugged his shoulders.

After a while, they turned and walked back in the direction of Nissim's house. As they came to a large house, the old man said, "This is a pleasant house, but I wonder if there are living creatures in this house."

Nissim could no longer restrain himself. He laughed and said, "This is my house. Come in and rest awhile. Refresh yourself with a cup of coffee and see for yourself if the people are living." Nissim hoped the old man would accept his invitation so that perhaps he would explain the strange remarks he had made during their walk.

The old man entered the house and gratefully accepted a cup of coffee. Drinking the strong coffee, Nissim was also refreshed, as he had not rested for these past two days thinking of how to solve the riddle of the *shammash*.

He turned to his guest and asked, "What did you mean by your remark about living creatures when we reached my house?"

And the old man smiled, saying, "Living creatures means children. And when there are children who are full of joy and life, and the parents bring them up with the love of Torah, then the children keep their joy of life forever."

When Nissim heard this, his heart was filled with a happy feeling and he answered, "Baruch haShem, Blessed be God for He has given us beautiful children, but they are asleep now."

Now Nissim was more assured that the stranger was not out of his mind, but rather filled with a deep wisdom. And so he continued to question the old man.

"Your words puzzled me, my friend. What did you mean when we passed the wheat field and you wondered whether the crop had already been eaten?"

And the old man answered, "Some people spend more than they earn, so I wondered if the people who owned the wheat field had debts they would have to pay with the crop. Thus, the crop would belong to someone else even before it is reaped."

"I understand. And what did you mean by asking if the man in the coffin was alive or dead? That seems to be an obvious choice," asked Nissim cautiously.

"Not at all. You see, when a person lives like a man and not like an animal, when he studies Torah and keeps the commandments and does good deeds, then he lives forever. His good deeds and acts of loving-kindness live after him. When his body dies, his soul survives and continues to live in eternal life. People remember him for good. In Safed, the righteous are buried in that part of the cemetery called *Beit HaHaim*, the House of the Living. And so the wicked are dead even in their lifetime, but the righteous, even after their death, are called 'living.'"

Now Nissim came to the one remaining question. "What did you mean when you asked who would carry whom? That didn't seem to make any sense at all."

The old man laughed a little and answered, "When people travel together, and the way seems long and hard, they tell stories or sing songs, or have a discussion on a point of Talmud. Then the way seems shorter and the traveling lighter, as though one traveler were carrying the other. So what I was asking was who will begin telling something interesting to the other?"

What appeared to be so mysterious to Nissim a few moments before now became so easy to understand. He also apologized to the old man for thinking that he was perhaps foolish or even mad.

Then they sat in silence. After a while, the old man leaned over and said to Nissim, "I see that something is troubling your soul. As Solomon said, 'A man should speak of the anxiety in his heart to help lighten it.'"

Sensing that this man had the power to understand, Nissim thought that perhaps he could help him with his problem. He then told the man about the Sultan's visit and his command to appear before him to explain the secret of the *shammash*. "I tried to explain about the *shammash* to the Sultan, but he accused me of withholding something from him. What can I tell him tomorrow? What secret does the *shammash* contain?"

The old man sat for a moment, looking as though he

had been expecting this question. "Tell the Sultan that this is the secret of the *shammash*. The *shammash* stands up high to look out and announce the following: 'Everyone look at me. I was once stored in a juicy fruit called the olive. When I grew and almost burst, I called out, "Pick me, put me into an olive press, take my oil to the last drop so I can live and be useful." So they came and plucked me from the tree, put me into the olive press, threw away my outer skin, and saved my inner part, my soul. And now I burn with a happy light that drives away darkness. Learn from me.' And so we must do what *shammash* tells us. We must help to spread Torah and light. We must help the weak and oppressed. We must help the needy and teach those who do not know. In this way, you will also rise to a higher level and the world will benefit from you."

As Nissim listened, tears appeared in his eyes and he wept. After a while, he raised his head and turned to thank the old man. But he had vanished. "He must have been Elijah the Prophet," Nissim said with wonder and a grateful heart.

Now that he had learned the secret of the *shammash*, he could go to the Sultan with the answer to his question.

A MELODY IN ISRAEL: AN ISRAELI TALE

"So what silly tune did you compose now, Dovid? Let me hear it and I'll tell you if you should sing it at the Hanukkah party in front of all those people."

"It's not a silly tune at all, Leahle," answered Dovid. "And I won't sing it for you now. No wonder your parents call you a *brenfire*. That's what you are."

"You know I'm only teasing you. Come on, do sing it. Or just play it on the piano and hum it. I won't say a word until you are through. I promise."

"All right," agreed Dovid eagerly. "Listen. It's a duet. I wrote it in honor of Hanukkah. I used the words of *Haneiros Halalu*. We kindle these lights because of the wondrous deliverance. You performed for our ancestors. I'll sing the first line, then like an echo, you'll sing the second line. Then we join our voices in harmony on *al ha nissim*." Then with great delight, Dovid sat at the piano and began to play and sing his new composition.

Leah came closer and began to read the notes and sing with Dovid, and soon their voices grew stronger and

surer—blending, harmonizing, joining together rhyth-
mically. When they had finished, Dovid stood up and
gave Leah a hug—and just as suddenly jumped back.
"Forgive me, Leahle, I didn't mean to hug you. I mean, I
should not have done that. I was just so happy to hear
my song come to life, like when we first light the
Hanukkah candles. It's so beautiful, isn't it? Do you think
so too, Leahle?"

Leah stood there, wanting to laugh, wanting to tease
Dovid about the song, about the hug, even about his
apology, but somehow, no sound came from her moving
lips. Only the words, "Oh my beloved. The voice of my
beloved!" came into her mind. She kept looking into
Dovid's eyes, seeing him in a new way. The words of
Song of Songs kept repeating in her mind. *"Behold, you
are fair, my love, Behold, you are fair with your eyes as
doves. And, oh, you are handsome, my lover, oh, sweet."*

And Dovid, too, kept looking at Leah. He understood
what Solomon meant when he wrote, *"How fair is your
love, my sister, my bride."* But he was also confused.

Leah had been like a sister all his life. They had known
each other from the time they had been little children.
Their houses were on the same street in their Eastern
European town. They went to the same *heder*. Dovid
loved music and they often sang together. Dovid was in
the choir at the *shul*, and although girls were not
permitted to sing with the cantor and his choir, Leah
learned all the melodies from listening and practicing
with Dovid at home.

As Dovid grew older, he began writing down the
melodies that were in his head with the help of his piano
teacher and the cantor. Now Dovid could write his own

music, even with piano chords. Dovid always shared his ideas and his music, and sometimes even his feelings, with his friend Leah. They had never thought about love . . . that is, not until now. And still they kept their thoughts to themselves. They did not want words to disturb this holy silence.

Weeks went by and it was Hanukkah, the 25th day of Kislev, 5701 (1940). Dovid and Leah were returning from the Hanukkah party at the *shul*. Dovid and the choir had sung his duet, but it was really Leah who sang it with him, although only from the audience. All week there was news about the war, and rumors that the Jews would soon be rounded up and put into a ghetto, or worse, sent to work camps. Everyone tried to find out what was going to happen, what they must do to save their families, their children. And still, at Hanukkah, the Jews gathered to light the *menorah*, recite the blessing, and sing the songs of hope and miracle, praying with fervor, *"Not by might, nor by power, but by My spirit alone shall we all live in peace."* This was a time when those words from Zacharias, and the story of Hanukkah, meant even more to every Jew.

By the end of the festival, Dovid and Leah had learned that they would be separated, for they were to go into hiding with their own families. Who knew when or how they would ever meet again? They knew, though, that their love for each other would continue.

The day after Hanukkah they met to talk, perhaps for the last time. Dovid picked up his wooden and brass *menorah* and said, "Leahle, I will cut this *menorah* in half. You take one half and I'll take the other. Let's keep our halves with us always, to remind us of our love that was kindled at the beginning of this *yom tov*. Let's hope and pray, *tiere* Leahle, that we can see each other soon again in freedom and peace. Then we can sing our duet as we light our candles together as husband and wife." Leah pledged her love to Dovid, and he cut the *menorah* in half, giving one half to Leah and keeping the other for himself.

Soon after, the war came, and Leah and her family fled to Russia. All during the war Leah kept the half-*menorah* in her pocket, and when she looked at it, she felt the closeness to Dovid. All this time she did not hear any news from him. Still, she dreamed of meeting Dovid— she didn't know how or where—and of bringing the two halves of the *menorah* together. Maybe next Hanukkah, she secretly hoped.

Leah often sang, but not the joyous songs that Dovid wrote, only the plaintive songs of the Jewish people. And especially when she felt loneliness or despair, she sang *"Dovdl, du lebst in mayn zikorn*. Dovidl, you live in my memory."

Dovid and his parents fought with the Partisans through-out the war. He, too, kept the *menorah* in his pocket, always checking to make sure it had not dropped out as he ran through the forests to escape from the enemy. Every time he touched it, he felt renewed courage and hope.

Finally the war was over. Joining thousands of other Jewish survivors, Dovid and his parents walked across Europe, across snow-filled mountains and steep rocky paths, on their way to Italy. It was April 1946. When they arrived at a small port in Italy, the immigrants found a ship, hired by the Mossad emissaries, waiting for them.

They crowded onto the ship and sailed to Milan. Then the immigrants, each supplied with false papers, food, and clothing, waited until dark. Using British Army vehicles as a front, they were driven to some dark, secret inlet on the Mediterranean where a boat was waiting to take them to the Land of Israel.

By dawn, the ship was on its way to the east, with the Jewish flag flying from the mast and the Jews on board singing *Hatikva*, first in Yiddish and then in Hebrew.

After a day at sea, Dovid's heart began to feel new life. He often sang for the people on the ship, songs in Yiddish, but also many Hebrew songs he had learned, with Leah, as part of the Zionist Youth Movement. He sang "Song of the Sea." He was traveling to a new land, his people's land, to a place where he didn't know what would happen, but where he could begin afresh. The first thing he would do when he arrived would be to give himself a new name, a new *mazal*. He knew the name he would choose, Uri, light. He carried always within his heart Leah's fire, and, in his pocket, his half of the *menorah*. That he would not leave behind.

It was a time when the British ruled Palestine. They patrolled the Haifa shore with boats and guns, knowing that illegal Jewish immigrants were attempting to arrive. But all this did not discourage the Jews from trying, and they were successful many times over. The landings always had to be carried out at night, with no lights so as not to give the British any cause for suspicion. On shore, Ze'ev Hayam, the first Jewish naval captain, organized the rescue parties. The Haganah agents maintained radio contact with the refugee boat and guided it to the safest place, especially to avoid British patrols. Ze'ev Hayam waited for word that the ship had arrived, and which spot had been picked for taking the passengers from the ship. Then he signaled his men to begin the rescue. All the people held their breath hoping that the British would not be alerted and drive the ship back to Europe. The people on the boat also prayed that they would land safely on the shores of Haifa and not have to spend even more miserable days on that boat to return . . . to what?

It was quiet, except for the sound of the waves of the sea. The signal came at last. The waiting men began to move, and like a choreographed dance, they walked into the waters of Bat Galim, toward the boat. They walked into the water up to their chins, forming a man-made bridge of shoulders. Then the people left the boat and walked on these men's shoulders until they reached the shallow waters and the sandy beach, the land. Women and men, doctors and nurses, were waiting there, each one taking someone, a man or woman or child who had just come from the boat. Quietly, quickly, they whisked them away, smuggling them to their homes.

The next day, the British began looking for the people from the boat. No one knew anything about them. "Of course not. People landing at Bat Galim? Really? That's not possible. No, I haven't seen anyone. I was home asleep."

After a few days, the Jews from Europe were rested, received a new set of false papers and new clothes and were then reunited with their families. Dovid, or rather Uri, was reunited with his parents and they began to make a new life for themselves, not only learning the language, adjusting to the new climate, and meeting new people, but also seeking out their *landsleit* from Eastern Europe.

Uri searched everywhere and asked everyone he met about Leah. He followed every lead he heard about. But no one knew anything. Some people tried to give him hope that he would find her. Others just shrugged their shoulders and lowered their eyes, not saying a word. Everyone was looking for a loved one. Survivors were scattered all over the world.

All this time Uri was becoming an Israeli. He learned to speak Hebrew, he attended school, he fought in the War of Independence, and then decided to become a cantor. He loved Haifa, his first home in the Jewish state. As he walked down and up the hills, he could smell the beautiful fragrance of jasmine. He would look and see everywhere the stately cedars and graceful cypresses. But he saw them through a veil of tears as he recited, "'*The beams of our house are cedar, cypresses are our rafters.*' Oh, Leahle, oh, my beloved." And Uri would quickly run to a place where he could weep for his beloved Leah in solitude.

Uri often sang for the people at the old age home, especially the songs in Yiddish that they remembered. Hearing those songs helped bring them closer to their homes, to the people they remembered, to the life that was never to be again. They lived with their memories and they loved the sweet voice of their cantor. The home was on the Carmel, looking down on Bat Galim, the beach where Uri had first arrived in Israel.

He started visiting the people there just before Rosh Hashanah that year, 1948, when Israel became a State. It was a strange little lady he met at the synagogue who brought him there. She said to him, "Cantor, we need to hear those songs to keep the spark of our Jewishness alive. Come sing for us." She sat there that first day, wearing a bonnet and wrapped in a large flowered shawl and smiling all the while as he sang. And though he went there at least once a week, he never saw her there again. When he asked about her, no one seemed to know her. It was as if she had disappeared into thin air.

It was Hanukkah in Israel. Uri was on the way to the old age home to help the people there celebrate the *yom tov* by chanting the blessings over the first candle and singing a concert of holiday songs. As he was crossing the little crooked street, he looked up at the star-filled sky, remembering another first night of Hanukkah, and then he saw something in a window. He thought perhaps he was still retaining the image of the stars and he blinked hard and looked again. He thought he saw half a *menorah* made of wood and brass. He must be imagining it, he thought. Perhaps the curtain was draped over the other half. There was one candle lit in it, but after all it was hard to see what it really was when it was so dark.

That night, Uri could not sleep well. He dreamed that he was there with Leah, in his house, playing the piano and singing *Haneiros Halalu*. He had not sung that duet since they had had to part, since the night he separated the *menorah* in half.

In the morning, he woke with a start. "Should I perhaps go to that house and ask, 'How did you get that half-*menorah*?' They'll think I'm crazy. 'Half-*menorah*, Cantor? No one lights only half a *menorah*.'" All day long, Uri was in a daze. He could not concentrate on his work. He went to the synagogue, but did not know what he was doing. Finally, he was determined to go back that night, to pass the house again, and see whether what he had noticed the night before was really there. If not, then he would know that he had imagined it. They say that if you really want to see something, it will appear. The mind can play tricks.

That day seemed to last a thousand hours. Finally, it was almost dark. He walked slowly to that street. He kept from looking at the stars. Instead he looked directly up at the window. It was there, but this time with two candles. He stood there frozen, his mind wanting to believe, to hope, but . . . what if he were to be disappointed? Maybe someone had found the *menorah*. . . . He stopped thinking about it, and knocked on the door. The door was slightly ajar. A woman's voice called out in Hebrew, "*Yavo*—Come in."

It is the voice of my beloved, thought Uri. Without thinking, yet not wanting to scare her, he began to sing softly the first line, "*Haneiros halalu onu madlikin.*" Then he stopped, and just as softly her voice echoed back, "*Haneiros halalu onu madlikin.*"

All during the week of Hanukkah, Uri and Leah talked about what had happened to them since their last time together. But at times they shared only silence between them. Leah spoke about the years in Russia and how she and her family, at the end of the war, arrived in Israel with the help of the Jewish Agency. Then she added, in a teasing voice, "You may have come by ship to Eretz Yisrael, Dovidl, but we came by an underground railroad, which I helped dig with my half of the *menorah*."

"Well, I helped row the ship with my half of the

menorah," Dovid retorted. And they both laughed in a way that they had not in years.

Suddenly Leah stopped laughing and said quietly, "Dovid, I've just had a strange memory. I just remembered an old woman who was with us as we left Russia. One day, as we were walking through a village, my part of the *menorah* dropped from my pocket. This woman—I don't even know her name. All I recall is that she wore a wonderful large shawl and she had a smile that filled my heart with hope—picked up the *menorah*. As she handed it back to me, she said, almost like a blessing, "You will find your destined love in Israel." I wonder who she was and where she is now. I would like to thank her and invite her to our wedding."

"Was it a big, *flowered* shawl?" asked Dovid.

"Yes," answered Leah with surprise. "How did you know that?"

Dovid gave Leah a hug and danced with her around the room, singing loudly and laughing, at the same time.

"Dovid! Dovid! What is it? Do you know this woman? Tell me, Dovid, how you knew she wore a flowered shawl," Leah demanded. But Dovid kept singing and dancing without answering.

Finally, out of breath, he said, "Leahle, that old woman was Sarah Bat Tuvim. I'm sure of it. The woman you met and the woman who invited me to sing at the old age home are the same woman. It was Sarah Bat Tuvim. Don't you remember reading about her in folk tales when we were children? She helps arrange marriages, a sort of *shadchente*, who also had a habit of vanishing. And it was she who brought us together in Israel."

Uri and Leah, who decided to call herself Orah, which

also means light, got married on the eighth night of Hanukkah. Uri brought to the wedding his half of the *menorah*. Orah brought her half also. This was the gift they gave to each other. For the first time since that night so long ago, they lit the candles on their *menorah*, fitted together to make it whole, and sang the blessings, adding the *shehecheyanu*. Then the beloveds began to sing *Haneiros Halalu*, their voices weaving together the joy they were feeling in their hearts. As they were singing, Orah and Uri looked out at a table near the door. One woman was sitting there, alone. She was wearing a flowered shawl and a bonnet—and she was smiling.

GLOSSARY OF TERMS

Al HaNissim: A special prayer for Hanukkah in which God is thanked for wondrous miracles.

Antiochus: The Syrian King who forbade the Jews to practice their religion.

Chag HaUrim: The Festival of Lights, another name for Hanukkah.

Dreidel: A four-sided top used in a Hanukkah Game. In Hebrew, it's called a "sevivon."

Elazar: A famous scribe who died as a martyr for his religion at the hands of the Syrians.

Emmaus: The place where the Jews gained a major victory over the Syrians.

Hallel: Psalms of praise recited on Hanukkah.

Hanerot Halallu: A Hanukkah hymn sung after the candle lighting.

Hannah: A brave Jewish woman whose seven sons died for their religion.

Hanukkah Gelt: Money given to children as a gift on Hanukkah.

Hanukkiah: The Hebrew name for a Hanukkah menorah.

Hellenists: Those Jews who sided with the Syrian-Greeks and adopted Greek ways and customs.

High Priest: The priest in charge of the service in the Temple in Jerusalem.

Judah: The son of Mattathias. As general of the Jewish armies, he led the Jews to final victory over the Syrians.

Latkes: Potato pancakes, a favorite Hanukkah food. In Hebrew, they are called "levivot."

Maccabee: The name given to Judah and later to his family and descendants.

"Maoz Tzur": One of the popular hymns sung after the lighting of the Hanukkah candles.

Mattathias: The old priest, father of Judah, who first started the war against the Syrians.

Modin: Home of Mattathias and his family and the town where the war against the Syrians began.

Nun, Gimel, Hay, and Shin: The Hebrew letters on the dreidel.

Shamash: The special servant candle used to light the others.

Tevet: The Hebrew month in which Hanukkah ends.

FOR FURTHER READING

Bloch, Abraham P. (1978). *The Biblical and Historical Background of the Jewish Holy Days*. New York: Ktav Publishers.

Epstein, Morris, and Schloss, Ezekiel (1968). *World Over Story Books*. New York: Bloch Publishing Company.

Frankel, Ellen (1989). *The Classic Tales*. Northvale, New Jersey: Jason Aronson.

Ganzfried, Solomon (1961). *Code of Jewish Law*. New York: Hebrew Publishing Company.

Gaster, Theodor H. (1953). *Festivals of the Jewish Year*. New York: William Morrow and Company.

Golumb, Morris (1973). *Know Your Festivals and Enjoy Them*. New York: Shengold.

Greenberg, Irving (1988). *Living the Jewish Way*. New York: Summit Books.

Isaacs, Ronald H., and Olitzky, Kerry M. (1994). *Sacred Celebrations: A Jewish Holiday Handbook*. New Jersey: Ktav Publishers.

Isaacs, Ronald H. (1989). *The Jewish Family Game Book for the Sabbath and Festivals*. New Jersey: Ktav Publishers.

Klein, Isaac (1979). *A Guide to Jewish Religious Practice*. New York: Jewish Theological Seminary.

Marcus, Eliezer, and Rush, Barbara (1980). *Seventy and One Tales for the Jewish Year*. New York: A.Z.Y.F.

Raphael, Chaim (1972). *A Feast of History*. New York: Gallery Books.

Schram, Peninnah, and Rosman, Steven M. (1990). *Eight Tales for Eight Nights*. Northvale, New Jersey: Jason Aronson.

Strassfeld, Michael (1985). *The Jewish Festivals*. Philadelphia: Jewish Publication Society.

Vainstein, Yaacov (1964). *The Cycle of the Jewish Year*. Jerusalem: World Zionist Organization.

Waskow, Arthur (1982). *Seasons of our Joy: A Handbook of Jewish Festivals*. New York: Summit Books.

INDEX

171

About the Author

Rabbi Ronald H. Isaacs has been the spiritual leader of the Temple Sholom in Bridgewater, NJ, since 1975. He received his doctorate in instructional technology from Columbia University's Teachers College. He is the author of more than sixty books. His most recent publications include *Every Person's Guide to Death and Dying in the Jewish Tradition* and *Every Person's Guide to Jewish Philosophy and Philosophers.* Rabbi Isaacs currently serves as chairperson of the publications committee of the Rabbinical Assembly of America and, with his wife, Leora, designs and coordinates the adult learning summer experience called Shabbat Plus at Camp Ramah in the Poconos. He resides in New Jersey with his wife, Leora, and their children, Keren and Zachary.

Recommended Resources